Inquietus
LaSalle in the Illinois Country

CENTER FOR FRENCH COLONIAL STUDIES
CENTRE POUR L'ETUDE DU PAYS DES ILLINOIS
WILLIAM L. POTTER PUBLICATION SERIES

THE CENTER FOR FRENCH COLONIAL STUDIES, INC.

WILLIAM L. POTTER PUBLICATION SERIES

SERIES EDITOR, BENN E. WILLIAMS

The Center for French Colonial Studies (CFCS)

Founded in 1983, the Center for French Colonial Studies, also known as the Centre pour l'étude du pays des Illinois, promotes and encourages research into the social, political, and material history of the French colonies and French people of the Middle Mississippi Valley and the Midwest, with special focus on the Illinois Country in the seventeenth, eighteenth, and early nineteenth centuries. CFCS is organized as a 501(c)(3) corporation for exclusively charitable, literary, scientific and educational purposes. In now its third decade, the membership continues to consist of historians, archeologists, preservation technologists, architectural historians, genealogists, historic interpreters, and interested laypeople.

The William L. Potter Publication Series

The dissemination of knowledge forms an integral part of the organization's mission. One means to this end is the annual autumnal meeting and conference; another is the publication of the quarterly *Le Journal*, which emphasizes original research, book reviews, announcements, and news relating to the Center's mission. Recognizing a "publications gap" between shorter articles and monograph-length works, CFCS initiated its *Extended Publications Series* in order to make additional scholarship available to the public. This program publishes essays, monographs, and translations of primary documents that might not otherwise enjoy a place in print owing to their in-between length or esoteric nature. The name of the series was changed in 2011 to honor the memory of longtime series editor, board member, and past president William L. Potter.

The Voyageur in the Illinois Country: The Fur Trade's Professional Boatmen in Mid America
    Margaret K. Brown

Jean-Baptiste Cardinal and the Affair of Gratiot's Boat: An Incident in the American Revolution
    Robert C. Wiederaenders

Louis Lorimier in the American Revolution, 1777-1782: A Mémoire by an Ohio Indian Trader and British Partisan
    Paul L. Stevens

Code Noir: The Colonial Slave Laws in French Mid-America [Bilingual edition]
    William Potter, editor; B. Pierre Lebeau, translator; and a preface by Carl J. Ekberg

French Colonial Studies: Le Pays des Illinois; Selections from Le Journal, 1983-2005
    Margaret K. Brown and H. Randolph Williams, editors

*Plumbing the Depths of the Upper Mississippi Valley. Julien Dubuque, Native Americans, and Lead Mining
    With Annotated, Transcribed, and Translated Original Documents*
    B. Pierre Lebeau; Lucy Eldersveld Murphy; Robert C. Wiederaenders

Standing up for Indians: Baptism Registers as an Untapped Source for Multicultural Relations in St. Louis, 1766-1821
    Sharon Person

The French Colony in the Mid-Mississippi Valley (2nd ed.)
    Margaret Kimball Brown and Lawrie Cena Dean

Massacre 1769: The Search for the Origin of the Legend of Starved Rock
    Mark Walczynsk

Franco-American Identity, Community and La Guiannée (co-publication with the University Press of Mississippi)
    Anna Servaes

Inquietus
LaSalle in the Illinois Country

Mark Walczynski

CENTER FOR FRENCH COLONIAL STUDIES
CENTRE POUR L'ETUDE DU PAYS DES ILLINOIS
WILLIAM L. POTTER PUBLICATION SERIES
NUMBER 12

THE CENTER FOR FRENCH COLONIAL STUDIES, INC.
3308 Preston Road, Suite 350 #348,
Plano, TX 75093-7471
www.frenchcolonialstudies.org
frenchcolonialstudies@gmail.com

Series editor: Benn E. Williams

ISBN-13: 978-1-7340354-0-7 (paper)
ISBN-13: 978-1-7340354-1-4 (electronic)

Front cover: Detail of Jean Baptiste Louis Franquelin's Carte de l'Amerique Septentrionnale: depuis le 25, jusqu'au 65⁰ deg. de latt. & environ 140, & 235 deg. de longitude [1688] Map. Public Domain, https://www.loc.gov/item/2002622264/.

Title page: La Salle, http://www.ifremer.fr/envlit/actualite/20030401.htm, Public Domain, https://commons.wikimedia.org/w/index.php?curid=25673.

Library of Congress Control Number:2019950059
Library of Congress Cataloguing-in-Publication Data
A catalog record for this book is available from the Library of Congress.

Text composed in Georgia

To my late parents, Sylvester and Rita Walczynski.

CONTENTS

TABLE OF ILLUSTRATIONS   ix

INTRODUCTION   1

CHAPTER 1
THE FRENCH ARRIVE IN THE ILLINOIS COUNTRY   9

CHAPTER 2
RAPIDS, FORKS, AND BARKS   19

CHAPTER 3
SETTING THE RECORD STRAIGHT,
MICHILIMACKINAC, AND THE IROQUOIS   47

CHAPTER 4
LA SALLE REGROUPS, 1681-1682   57

CHAPTER 5
LA SALLE ILLINOIS COUNTRY HEADQUARTERS
AT LE ROCHER, STARVED ROCK   69

CHAPTER 6
LA SALLE'S ILLINOIS COUNTRY LEGACY   99

BIBLIOGRAPHY   107

ABOUT THE AUTHOR   113

ILLUSTRATIONS

Figure 1:   Marquette meets the Illinois Indians   9

Figure 2:   Louis Jolliet as portrayed at the Starved Rock State Park
                Visitor Center   12

Figure 3:   A model of what La Salle's Griffon may have looked like   15

Figure 4:   Illinois River Rapids at Marseilles, Illinois   19

Figure 5:   Image of Franquelin's 1675 map, also known as La Frontenacie,
                based on information provided by Louis Jolliet   23

Figure 6:   Site of the Grand Village of the Illinois   25

Figure 7:   Sheer St. Peter Sandstone cliffs covered with eastern white pine
                and cedar are typical of the Starved Rock area   30

Figure 8:   La Salle's Fort de Crèvecoeur   31

Figure 9:   Marquette's 1673 map depicts Otoe and Peoria villages located
                at or near today's Des Moines River   33

Figure 10:   Starved Rock and the frozen Illinois River   35

Figure 11:   The shallow and rocky Vermilion River in the vicinity of where
                the Shawnee encountered the Iroquois war party in September 1680   41

Figure 12:   Father Ribourde monument located at St. Patrick's Catholic Church
                in Seneca, Illinois   46

Figure 13:   Franquelin's 1675 map depicting Europeans at the Gulf and
                the Mosopela (M8hs8peria)   51

Figure 14:   A pirogue or dugout canoe   59

Figure 15:   The Mississippi River at the Gulf of Mexico as seen from the air.   64

Figure 16:   Today's Starved Rock, site of La Salle's Fort St. Louis.   68

Figure 17:   Today's Plum Island   70

Figure 18:   A model of La Salle's Fort St. Louis at the Starved Rock State Park
                Visitor Center   72

Figure 19:   Blacksmiths were important members of the French group
                at Fort St. Louis   74

Figure 20:   A photograph of the second of two Peoria village sites reported by Jacques Marquette   77

Figure 21:   Detail of Jean-Baptiste Franquelin's 1684 *Carte de la Louisiane* map depicting La Salle's Indian colony in present-day northern Illinois   80

Figure 22:   The sandstone promontory known as the Little Rock   90

Figure 23:   One of the paleo-channels located between bluffs at Starved Rock State Park and the Illinois River   91

Figure 24:   Buffalo Rock as seen from the frozen Illinois River   101

Figure 25:   1867 US Army Corps of Engineers map depicting Fort St. Louis at a site south of Starved Rock   102

Figure 26:   The Illinois and Michigan Canal at La Salle, Illinois   104

Figure 27:   Crest of the USS La Salle (AGF-3)   105

INTRODUCTION

René-Robert Cavelier, a seventeenth-century French adventurer, later known simply as La Salle, was a seminal figure in Canadian, American, and early Illinois history. He envisioned a waterborne highway that would extend from the St. Lawrence Valley to the Gulf of Mexico, one that he could use to further trade and enhance his enterprise. He planned to bring the tribes of the upper Mississippi, the Illinois Country, and points beyond into his trade network. Though he was not the first European to visit Illinois lands, he was the first to attempt to incorporate the natural resources, indigenous people, and lands and waters of the territory into the larger paradigm of French colonization, settlement, and commerce. This remarkable long view is oftentimes tainted by historians who have viewed the explorer as a schemer, egotistical madman, or the Great Man who shaped events and literally cast the unfolding historical narrative himself. For the last 150 years, much of this misunderstanding has adversely impacted both Cavelier's reputation and his accomplishments. This narrative will leave the reader with reliable information from which to base his or her own conclusions.

Born in Rouen, in northern France, to a wealthy upper-middle-class family of wholesale merchants, in 1643, Cavelier received a Jesuit education, intending one day to enter the priesthood. At fourteen, he began his novitiate in Paris. There, Cavelier was introduced to Ignatius Loyola's *Spiritual Exercises*, spending many days in prayer and meditation, searching his soul to learn if indeed, he had been called to the Order by God. Successfully completing this two-year phase of his training, he pledged his initial vows of the Order, becoming an "approved scholastic." Cavelier then began a three-year course of instruction in philosophy, a subject that included logic, physics, metaphysics, and mathematics, the latter being an umbrella term that included geography, astronomy, and hydrography. According to Jesuit historian Gilbert Garraghan:

> The use of the globes and of the quadrant and other measuring instruments was taught. The importance assumed by the physical sciences and mathematics in the Le Flèche and Paris [Jesuit universities'] curriculum was due largely to the presence in these schools of numerous sons of the nobility who were looking forward to a career in the army or navy.[1]

These important subjects would later come in handy while he traversed the Great Lakes and the rivers and lands of the Illinois Country, skills to which Henri Joutel, the chronicler of the explorer's 1684 Texas expedition, readily vouched.[2]

Cavelier was described by one of his earlier Jesuit mentors as "Exuberantly healthy, big-sized, lusty, proud, impressionable, stubborn, domineering, [and] hot-tempered," attributes that would later become prerequisites for leading rugged woodsmen through the Illinois wilderness and for persuading fickle tribesmen to ally

---

[1] Gilbert J. Garraghan, S.J., "La Salle's Jesuit Days," *Mid-America magazine* XIX (1937): 95.
[2] Ibid., 96.

with him rather than acquiesce to the cajoling or intimidation of others.[3] He was also touted for his "excellent ability" and "talent for mathematics."[4] Cavelier was a polyglot. Even before he entered the Jesuit novitiate, he was conversant in Spanish, soon learned Greek, and, while he studied and taught at the various Jesuit colleges, he became "fairly well versed" in Arabic and Hebrew. It is also likely that, as an aspiring Catholic priest, he knew Latin.[5]

Between 1662 and 1666, he taught the equivalent of second, third, and fourth year high school at Jesuit institutions in Alençon, Tours, and Blois. Yet he yearned for more than teaching young students. Aware of his skills, and possibly his own self-importance, Cavelier longed to use his talents in mission-fields such as China, where, eighty-years prior, the noted cartographer, mathematician, and Jesuit ambassador Matteo Ricci, the first western missionary to make inroads with Chinese intelligentsia, had attempted to establish a Chinese-Christian civilization.[6] Cavelier may have found himself caught up in a mid-seventeenth century debate occurring within the Order, a disagreement over how much missionaries should accommodate diverse native cultures and customs in light of Catholic teachings, on the one hand and to what extent the Society's missionaries should be involved in indigenous political dealings on the other. The boisterous Jesuit-in-training would have likely sided with the faction that supported Ricci, a man who believed that the Church should be flexible enough to understand and appreciate a culture's wisdom and then, with the knowledge of its symbolism and beliefs, attempt to Christianize it. Cavelier would later master the art of using symbolism to convince the Indians of Canada and of the Illinois Country to join him and participate in his wide-ranging enterprise.

Perhaps as a consequence of the Reformation and religious wars that engulfed Europe during the sixteenth-century century, and in conjunction with the role of the Order and their obedience to Church doctrine and council decrees, the Jesuits eventually sided not with the Ricci faction, but with the conservatives who put forth a restrained approach to missionary ingratiation to cultures in non-western lands. Given his brash temperament and eclectic interests, Cavelier may have felt slighted that the Jesuits did not support one of their own, especially one of Ricci's caliber. Perhaps knowing that, his views, like Ricci's, were atypical, Cavelier may have recognized potential difficulties regarding a career with the Order.[7]

Cavelier's unease with his circumstances began to manifest itself and eventually came to the attention of his Jesuit superiors, one of whom described him as "a poor student, self-opinionated, of very middling judgment and prudence." Similarly, another rector reported that Cavelier had "good talent, poor judgment [and] little prudence." A third described Cavelier as *inquietus*, or restless.[8]

---

[3] Ibid., 94.

[4] Ibid., 96.

[5] "Robert Cavelier to the General, Oliva, March 28, 1666," in Ibid., 101-103.

[6] "Matteo Ricci SJ (1552-1610)," Ignatian Spirituality, A Service of Loyola Press, accessed March 5, 2019 at URL: http://www.ignatianspirituality.com/ignatian-voices/16th-and-17th-century-ignatian-voices/matteo-ricci-sj.

[7] Ray Guthrie, PhD., Jesuit, personal communication, March 19, 2016.

[8] Garraghan, 96.

The Jesuits of the seventeenth-century could meld two divergent worlds into one formidable alliance that included the rich and powerful aristocracy *and* the people of the lowest socio-economic classes. The Order's upper echelon, including many of their most capable cardinals, bishops, rectors, professors, and other leaders, came from wealthy French families, who not only wielded enormous political and economic power, but also carried influence at the French court, with King Louis XIV, and with his ministers. At the time, the Order had established the finest schools in Europe, providing training for the aristocracy, the governing establishment, in science, logic, mathematics, and other intellectual fields. By contrast, the Order also ministered to the poor and uneducated masses, regardless of ethnicity, who were oblivious to the Gospel message, whose very souls were in the view of the Jesuits, doomed to perdition. By maintaining ties to the elite powerbrokers of French society and to the numbers of downtrodden masses, the Jesuits developed a very potent coalition that enabled them to influence the mighty and gain the support of the disadvantaged.

By March 1666, Cavelier's dissatisfaction with Jesuit life compelled him to trade the austere halls of the colleges to work in distant mission-fields. Using a tactic that Cavelier would later employ with the governor of Canada and the French court, Cavelier went to the top of the hierarchy to plead his case instead of expressing his concerns and aspirations to his immediate superiors. He wrote J.P. Oliva, General of the Order, "desiring and petitioning with the greatest eagerness," to be sent to China, explaining that his "zeal for souls" outweighed his "feebleness" for Jesuit university life. Eight days later, Cavelier wrote Oliva again, "pleading with great fervor" to be sent to Portugal, where he had heard that the Portuguese Jesuits had been seeking Greek and math instructors, two subjects in which he excelled. To make the plan more appealing to the Order, Cavelier offered that his family would pay his traveling expenses and donate 8,000 *livres* to the Chinese mission. Oliva's reply initially satisfied Cavelier. He commended the young priest-in-training for his zeal to labor in the foreign missions, but explained, by way of insinuation that Cavelier was neither emotionally nor spiritually equipped to undertake such an endeavor. The general did, however, acquiesce to Cavelier's entreaties by allowing him to abandon his teaching assignment and to begin his theological studies at La Flèche. The general's concession satisfied the young Jesuit for a short time only. In December, Cavelier again wrote to Oliva, begging the official to send him to Portugal, and once more adding the usual inducements to pay his own way and offering his family's support to the Portuguese mission. This time Oliva sternly instructed Cavelier to "remain quietly," and to finish his studies and serve his third probation; when those requirements had been met, Oliva would consider Cavelier's requests.[9]

This censure was more than Cavelier could bear. His impatience with the long process and tedious preparations necessary to become a full-fledged Jesuit, his inability to patiently accept his humble place within the Society, and his internal struggle that pit his talents against the consensus of the Order finally drove him to petition his superiors to be relieved of his vows. Cavelier's overseers soon forwarded written documentation, referencing his suitability to remain in the Order, to Rome. After examining Cavelier's

---

[9] Ibid.

dossier, Father J. Bordier, Provincial of Paris wrote Oliva to advise him that "his advisers" think it best to release Cavelier. On March 28, Cavelier officially left the Society and reentered secular life.[10]

Even though the Jesuit hierarchy agreed to release Cavelier from his vows, realizing that there was little hope of changing his restless nature, they did so with a touch of grace and dignity. Oliva wrote to Cavelier:

> Do you, my very dear Brother, wherever and whatsoever station of life you be, remember whence you have fallen and keep in mind the rock from which you have been cut away, and though separated in place, try to live ever in union of heart with us and with Jesus. His grace be always with you.[11]

Cavelier would never associate himself with the Order again, preferring the company of Recollect and Sulpician missionaries during his voyages. He would later develop an animus against the Jesuits in the West, especially for one particular missionary.

Upon his separation with the Order, Cavelier was confronted with facts that compelled him to leave for Canada and to begin anew. Cavelier had a good education for his time but had few employment prospects or business opportunities for applying his knowledge. Having been excluded from his family inheritance upon taking his Jesuit vows, he had little from which to draw support in France. Desirous of visiting new lands, as well as having kin in Canada, including a brother who was a Sulpician priest, and an uncle, Henri, who had been a member of the Company of One Hundred Associates (a private consortium of investors, merchants, government officials, and clerics organized to develop Canada's trade and establish settlement), Cavelier made the decision to travel to the colony.[12]

Cavelier's arrival in Canada coincided with an extended period of extraordinarily cool temperatures known commonly today as the Little Ice Age.[13] The Little Ice Age began to affect the Earth's northern hemisphere roughly during the mid-fourteenth century, and it continued into the mid-nineteenth. The coldest part of the Little Ice Age, a period known as the Maunder Minimum, occurred between 1645 and 1715, at the height of French exploration in North America. The cool temperatures affected plant life, in turn triggering changes in animal migrations, which, ultimately, caused the people who incorporated these animals into their material culture to follow the herds, sometimes relocating to new areas, and, if necessary, to develop new technologies. For the French in Canada, the cooler temperatures affected transportation, exploration, and westward expansion, as rivers and lakes were often frozen for extended periods. Cavelier experienced all these phenomena during his time in the Illinois Country. The

---

[10] Ibid.

[11] Ibid., 98.

[12] Céline Dupré, "Cavelier de La Salle, René Robert," *Dictionary of Canadian Biography* (Toronto: University of Toronto/Quebec: Université Laval, 1966, revised 2015), I:172 and Garraghan, 94.

[13] See Sam White, *A Cold Welcome: The Little Ice Age and Europe's Encounter with North America* (Cambridge: Harvard University Press, 2017).

temperatures also delayed and hampered communication between the colony and France. Although the French who lived in North America at the time did not realize that they were living in the midst of a climactic anomaly and did not understand the nature or extent of the influence of the cooler temperatures on the natural world, they likely believed that the cold was simply part of life in Canada.

A second and equally important precursor to La Salle's arrival in the colony was the period of relative peace that began in about 1666 between the French and the powerful Haudenosaunee, or Iroquois, a confederation of tribes composed of the Mohawk, Cayuga, Oneida, Onondaga, and Seneca, at that time commonly called the Five Nations. For over two decades, the Five Nations had menaced French interests in Canada.[14] The cessation of overt hostilities allowed the French to explore western lands, trade with western tribes, and to seek the religious conversion of the western Indians. This era of peace, coupled with Cavelier's knowledge and skills, created an opportunity for him just two years after he had arrived in the colony. The French Controller General of Finance and Minister of the marine Jean-Baptiste Colbert, and the French Intendent of Canada, Jean Talon, encouraged Cavelier to locate an inland water route that connected the St. Lawrence Valley to the southern or western sea, likely, in part, to circumvent the environmental conditions that kept the St. Lawrence River frozen for months at a time.[15] Although it is uncertain just how far Cavelier travelled during his first two expeditions, his exploits came to the attention of other Canadian officials, including Governor Louis de Buade, Comte de Frontenac et de Palluau (Frontenac), who eventually became Cavelier's most influential supporter. With Frontenac's recognition and support, the standing and status of Cavelier, who officially became known as La Salle, continued to grow.[16] As he had done when he was an aspiring Jesuit, La Salle felt that after having achieved what he believed were sufficient credentials, he sailed to France to petition Colbert for permission to reach the Gulf of Mexico by way of the Mississippi River. La Salle's request was approved by the court.

La Salle had chosen well the men who would form his inner circle including Henri Tonti, Michel Accault, Jacques Bourdon d'Autray, and François Dauphin de la Forêt. These were men whom La Salle trusted. Each possessed specific skills and thus performed different tasks and duties. The loosely knit team, La Salle hoped, would help him to accomplish his many objectives. To these men, La Salle would bestow titles,

---

[14] According to historian Tracy Neal Leavelle, "The Five Nations were better armed had a better supply of guns than their enemies because of their trading relationship with the Dutch, who were more willing than the French to trade firearms." Tracy Neal Leavelle, *The Catholic Calumet* (Philadelphia: University of Pennsylvania Press, 2012), 28.

[15] "Talon to the King" in Pierre Margry, *Découvertes et établissements des Français dans l'ouest et dans le sud de l'Amérique septentrionale, 1614-1754*, 6 vols. (Paris: Maisonneuve, 1875), I: 82, "Relation of l'Abbe de Galinee" in Margry, *Découvertes*, I: 113 and III: 285, and *La Salle, the Mississippi, and the Gulf, Three Primary Documents*, eds. Robert Weddle, Mary Christine Morkovsky, and Patricia Galloway (College Station: Texas A & M University, 1987), 31. French Minister of the Marine Jean Baptiste Colbert supported a reward to whomever discovered the mouth of the Mississippi. "M. Colbert to M. Talon" in *Documents Relating to the Colonial History of New York*, ed. Edmund Bailey O'Callaghan, 15 vols. on CD (Saugerties, NY: Hope Farm Press, 2001), IX: 89. Hereafter cited as O'Callaghan, *DCHNY*.

[16] See chapter one for information pertaining to Cavelier becoming La Salle.

authority, and land.[17] La Salle would continue "counting on a few loyal men," in the words of Patricia Galloway, when the explorer landed at Matagorda Bay, establishing the first French presence in present-day Texas.[18]

La Salle had to contend with scoundrels, who seemed invested in destroying him and derailing his enterprise. If a stern hand was required, La Salle could be a taskmaster, driving his men nearly to their breaking point; however, the explorer could also be compassionate, forgiving deserters and thieves for their crimes and reinstating them as contributing members of his group.

La Salle should not be seen as a friend of the Indian, although he was very aware that he needed them. He depended on the indigenous groups to help feed Tonti and the French during his absence from the Illinois Country in 1680, to accompany him to the Gulf in 1682, and to relocate to the upper Illinois Valley in 1683. He would befriend, cajole, threaten, or otherwise use any tribesman in any way he found them to be useful to him or his enterprise. Unlike the Jesuits and other missionaries, whose very existence among the tribes was predicated upon knowing their language, terminology, and customs, the explorer was not interested in the proper use of or recording terminology and was only interested in native customs if they helped him to further his aims.

From desertions to shipwrecks, Indian invasions to changes in colonial administration, and sickness to intrigue, La Salle seemed capable of adjusting to any circumstance. Nonetheless, La Salle clearly possessed human character flaws. Chief among them was his tendency to exaggerate, or embellish information, even to royal authorities. He also possessed no compunction about criticizing others, especially potential competitors or anyone whom he believed threatened his operations.

An astute observer of nature, La Salle carefully described the plains, cliffs, meadows, and valleys of the new lands. In his reports and correspondence, his observations included references to coal, limestone, slate, and hemp; he wrote about the local fauna and flora, even documenting the presence of exotic birds, such as "Perroquets" in today's Illinois. La Salle's reference to copper in the Illinois Valley may have inspired two eighteenth-century geological expeditions, one French (in 1722) and one British (in 1773). By the late nineteenth-century, corporations would begin mining the coal and limestone that the explorer mentioned in his reports.

When La Salle arrived in the Illinois Country in late 1679, his mission was to locate the Gulf of Mexico via the Mississippi River, and upon reaching the Gulf, to build a fort and warehouse to store heavy bison hides before they were transported to France. For this endeavor to be successful, many diverse aspects of the enterprise had to function simultaneously.[19] While traders purchased hides, other members of the group constructed forts. Others built sailing vessels, or kept the men fed. The enterprise

---

[17] La Salle awarded land grants to Jacques Bourdon d'Autray and Pierre Prudhomme and secured a commission for Tonti as captain of a company in the colonial troops. See *Early Narratives of the Northwest, 1634-1699*, ed. Louise Phelps Kellogg (New York: Scribner's Sons, 1917), 306.

[18] Weddle, Morkovsky, and Galloway, *Minet Relation*, 20.

[19] The size of the La Sallian enterprise depended on the time period and geography. When he entered Illinois in 1679, he had over 30 men in his group. Desertions dropped the number to six. He hired more men in 1680; however, the number is unknown. When La Salle left Illinois in 1683, there were between 17 and 20 men at Starved Rock. Native Americans in his employ were rather transient.

included individuals who carried supplies from one point to another, established cordial relations with the tribes, guarded property, or repaired guns. Other individuals managed La Salle's business affairs.[20] Given all aspects of the operation, it involved coordination across a nearly 1,000-mile stretch of North America, without the use of modern-day communication technology. While much of the coordination succeeded, La Salle, nonetheless, had to waste valuable time pursuing and arresting deserters, traveling to Montreal to borrow money, recruiting men, purchasing supplies, fighting Indians and illnesses, and brokering peace between warring tribes. Even more, amid this turmoil and across the wide expanse of land in North America, La Salle was allowed only five years to accomplish his charge of exploration of the waterways to the southern Gulf, construction of forts, and development of a successful trading operation.

Because La Salle had been forced to deal with one setback after the next, he was unable to reach the Gulf until April 1682, giving him only a little more than a year to finalize everything that he had planned to accomplish. He focused his attention on the upper Illinois Valley. With each passing day La Salle became more desperate to meet the terms of his patent; the methodical and deliberate La Salle became more audacious and hyperbolic.

Given his time constraints, he sought to persuade thousands of Indians to relocate their villages near his new headquarters in the west, his fort on Starved Rock. He left his Illinois Country fort in late August 1683 to petition the court for an extension of his patent so he could build that fort on the Gulf and see his western enterprise flourish.

La Salle's choice of the Illinois Country for his headquarters in the distant west was intentional. He knew that the Illinois River, even with its rapids and shoals, was still the most direct route from the Great Lakes to the Mississippi, and subsequently the Gulf of Mexico. Furthermore, the Illinois Indians, a large bison hunting tribe that lived along the stream, could deliver the peltry he sought. Above the confluence of the Illinois and Mississippi Rivers lived other bison-hunting tribes such as the Iowa and Otoe. This confluence of rivers and hunters would be a funnel for bison hides emanating from the Illinois Country and sent to the Gulf.

La Salle's understanding of the advantages afforded him in the Illinois Country were countered by known disadvantages. By allying with the Illinois, La Salle would anger the formidable Iroquois Confederacy, their staunch enemies. By establishing trade alliances with the western tribes and building a post on the Gulf, La Salle would become the enemy of the influential Montreal merchants whose livelihood was derived from hides traders who could potentially become La Salle's suppliers instead. Also, by building Fort St. Louis at Starved Rock and granting land to settlers in the Illinois Country, La Salle understood that he would provoke the ire of Canadian authorities, who had been instructed by the king to both discourage men from leaving the

---

[20] The size of the LaSallian enterprise depended on the time period and geography. When he entered Illinois in 1679, he had over thirty men in his group. Desertions dropped the number to six. He hired more men in 1680; however, the number though is unknown. When La Salle left Illinois in 1683, there were between seventeen and twenty men at Starved Rock. Native Americans in his employ were rather "transient."

settlements to trade with the Indians, and to consolidate Canada's population in the lower St. Lawrence Valley. By late 1682, these three powerful entities—he Iroquois, the merchants, and Canada's governor and intendent—would act to further their own agendas at Cavelier's expense.

La Salle was not able to complete what he sought to do in the Illinois Country. He accomplished even less during his next voyage, which ended in disaster in today's Texas. He had surrounded himself with competent men, but even these deputies could not shorten distances, halt Indian incursions, or change the hearts of conniving men, nor could La Salle fully manage the powerful political enemies he had made by developing a competing enterprise. He did succeed in laying the foundation of the Illinois fur trade and establishing the quintessential template for Franco-Native American relations, a remarkable achievement that was never replicated after his departure from the Illinois Country. Ultimately, without modern communication, La Salle's goals were thwarted by the very scope of the enterprise and the vast distances that the enterprise spanned.

CHAPTER ONE
THE FRENCH ARRIVE IN THE ILLINOIS COUNTRY

In May 1673, a fur trader named Louis Jolliet and a Jesuit missionary named Jacques Marquette, along with five other French adventurers, embarked on a voyage of discovery, to explore waterways that no European had yet seen. Leaving today's St. Ignace, Michigan, the crew paddled their canoes along the coast of Lake Michigan and ascended the Fox River at present-day Green Bay, Wisconsin. After completing the 2,700-step portage to the Wisconsin River, the group followed that stream to the Mississippi, a mysterious waterway that a delegation of Illinois Indians at the *Pointe du Saint Esprit* mission, near today's Ashland, Wisconsin, had described to Marquette and his predecessor, Claude-Jean Allouez.[1] Following the course of the Mississippi south, Jolliet and Marquette visited several Native American villages, some of which welcomed the French, while others sought to rob and kill them. Reaching an Indian village presumably located near the mouth of today's Arkansas River, Jolliet and Marquette discussed whether to continue down the Mississippi, or return north.[2] Having officially accomplished one of their mission's primary objectives—to determine where the waters of Mississippi River emptied, and fearing that they might be captured or detained by Spanish authorities, who had been seen in region, the two Frenchmen decided to retrace the Mississippi north toward Canada. Near today's Alton, Illinois, the French left the Mississippi and paddled up the Illinois River, becoming the first Europeans to navigate that stream. Proceeding up the Illinois, they stopped at a village that the French would call Kaskaskia, after the Illinois subtribe living there. Kaskaskia would become the focus of French missionaries, who strove to convert the Indians to Catholicism. Leaving Kaskaskia, the French continued their ascent of the Illinois, paddling along today's Des Plaines River. Local Indians showed them a portage that traversed a continental divide of mud to the Chicago River, and hence, to Lake Michigan. Heading north along the shorelines of today's Illinois and Wisconsin, the French canoes landed at the St. Francis Xavier mission, near today's Green Bay, Wisconsin. There, Marquette gave Jolliet his annual report to deliver to Canada's Jesuit Superior, Claude Dablon, documents that included a copy of his now famous journal and an accurate map of

---

[1] The Illinois Indians were an alliance of smaller subtribes that included the Kaskaskia, Peoria, Cahokia, Tamaroa, Espeminkia, Chinko, Coiracoetanon, Chepoussa, Tapouaro, Michigamea, and others who shared a similar language, culture, and oftentimes married outside of their sub-group.
[2] Jolliet and Marquette left the St. Ignace mission on May 17, 1673 and arrived at the Arkansas village just prior to July 17, traveling a distance of approximately 1,320 miles. *Jesuit Relations and Allied Documents, 1610-1791*, ed. Reuben Gold Thwaites (Cleveland: Burrows, 1901), LIX: 89, 159. On their journey down the Mississippi, they ventured about ten miles up the Des Moines River where they encountered two Peoria Indian villages, located at today's Illiniwek village State Historical site in Missouri. Ibid., 113-117.

the western lands and waters.[3] Jolliet departed the mission and paddled to his trade post located at Sault Ste. Marie, where he wintered. After the ice melted, he began the long journey to Quebec.

Jolliet and Marquette's journey, like that of Lewis and Clark in the nineteenth century, and that of Armstrong, Aldrin, and Collins in the twentieth, would become an important milestone in the exploration of new and uncharted worlds.

Figure 1: Marquette meets the Illinois Indians.
Photo from a display at the Starved Rock Visitor Center by the author.

Marquette returned to Kaskaskia, arriving at the village in April 1675, where he was reportedly received "as an angel from heaven" by the Illinois tribesmen. During his brief visit, Marquette personally visited Illinois cabins, twice performed Mass, and spoke as guest of honor to the assembled village chiefs and elders.[4] He also recorded important demographical data, noting that the village population had more than doubled, from approximately 1,450 people during his first visit in 1673, to more than 1,500 men alone.[5] Marquette and his two traveling companions, Jacques Largillier and Pierre Porteret, left the village shortly after Easter Sunday and headed for Michilimackinac, where the priest hoped to find some well-deserved rest from his long journey and to receive medical attention for a condition that would

---

[3] Raphael N. Hamilton, S.J., *Marquette's Explorations: The Narratives Reexamined* (Madison: University of Wisconsin Press, 1970), 4.

[4] Thwaites, LIX: 187.

[5] Marquette counted seventy-four cabins at the site for a population of about 1,450 people. Ibid. LIX: 159.

soon take his life. He never reached Michilimackinac, dying near present-day Ludington, Michigan.

Besides Marquette, Jesuit missionary Claude-Jean Allouez preached, taught, and ministered to the Illinois at Kaskaskia, arriving in the village in April 1677. Like Marquette, Allouez received a warm welcome from the Illinois who, shortly after his arrival, escorted him to his new abode, a cabin that, according to his hosts, had been where Marquette had lived two years earlier. Allouez gathered information about the village and its residents: walking through the site, he counted 351 cabins and a population of about 7,000 people.[6]

Allouez's first visit was brief as he came only to "acquire the information necessary for the establishment of a complete mission."[7] Still, the missionary baptized more than thirty-five people, primarily women and children, taught them prayers, and on the day of the Festival of the Holy Cross, watched his Illinois converts erect a cross thirty-five feet high in the middle of the village. About this event Allouez wrote:

> I can say in truth that they did not regard Jesus Christ Crucified as a folly, or a scandal; on the contrary, they assisted at that ceremony with great respect, and listened with admiration to all I had to say regarding that mystery. The children even came devoutly to kiss the Cross, while the grown-up people Earnestly entreated me to plant it there so firmly that it might never be in danger of falling.[8]

Allouez was content with the inroads he had made. To him it appeared that some were eager to learn, and many wanted their children baptized. Even if they had not converted to Catholicism, most of the Indians at Kaskaskia still respected him personally. Encouraged by these early achievements, Allouez believed that his mission would likely endure, possibly even flourish. Before leaving the village, the missionary entrusted his walking staff to the Illinois as a symbolic gesture of his presence among his new converts, a talisman that also assured them that he would return one day to retrieve it and renew their friendship.[9]

Despite his hard work and his relative success in converting, baptizing, and instructing the Indians, rumors of an impending Iroquois attack on the Illinois spread throughout the region. As we will see later in this narrative, Allouez may have helped to instigate it.

The Jesuit missionaries of Canada made enormous strides in the exploration of North America and in understanding its native people. Jogues, Allouez, Dablon, Marquette and others journeyed to places unknown to the French and established

---

[6] Allouez in Thwaites, LX: 157. The formula used by French missionaries to determine village populations are discussed in detail in "La Salle's Indian Colony" in chapter five.
[7] Ibid., 161.
[8] Ibid. 163-165.
[9] La Salle in *French Foundations*, Collections of the Illinois State Historical Library, vol. XXIII, French series Volume I, eds. Theodore Calvin Pease and Raymond C. Werner (Springfield: Trustees of the Illinois State Historical Library, 1934), 10-11.

working relations with the local tribes. They extended the boundaries of Canada beyond the scattered settlements of the St. Lawrence Valley by venturing into the Upper Great Lakes and into today's Illinois. While attempting to convert the Indians to Catholicism, the missionaries learned the local languages and customs. These proto-ethnographer Jesuits, many of whom came from wealthy and influential families, traded the comforts of France for a difficult transatlantic crossing to Canada and life in the wilderness. Thinking not of their own well-being, the missionaries worked tirelessly to save souls. They struggled daily against the powerful influence of village medicine men oftentimes subjecting themselves to mockery and even death, from the very people they sought to "save."

Figure 2: Louis Jolliet as portrayed at the Starved Rock State Park Visitor Center.
Photo by the author.

Having sacrificed mightily for their faith, the Jesuits believed that they had earned the right to influence the relations of future explorers and traders with western tribes like the Illinois. Despite their brief tenure, the missionaries had a sense of ownership of the lands where they ministered and loyalty to the Indians who lived there. With the foundation of their future endeavors firmly secured, the Jesuits resisted secular intrusion, believing that contact between French traders and the Indians would damage the relationships that the Jesuits had so arduously cultivated with the tribes. This concern was very real. On several occasions, tribal leaders summoned missionaries to curb the unruly behavior of French traders.[10]

Change was imminent. No longer would the Jesuits be the sole ambassadors of King Louis XIV and the Cross. A new group of men arrived, who would, in the eyes of the missionaries, negate much of their hard work. Leading this new contingent of explorers, traders, colonizers, and dreamers was René-Robert Cavelier. About Cavelier, historian Francis Parkman wrote, "The cravings of a deep ambition, the hunger of an insatiable intellect, the intense longing for action and achievement, subdued him in all other passions; and in his faults the love of pleasure had no part."[11] In 1667, Cavelier left his native France and sailed to Canada.

Arriving in Montreal, Cavelier quickly obtained a seigniory from the Sulpicians—a property along the south shore of the island; later Cavelier had his land cleared and a house constructed. Although it was considered poor social etiquette at the time, Cavelier, who was not yet a nobleman, began calling himself "La Salle," a grand sobriquet taken from his family's prestige in Rouen, France. Eager to explore new lands, Cavelier led two expeditions from Montreal, one in 1669 and another 1670. He planned to journey south and west into the wilderness with the intention of locating the passage to the south sea, and hence Mexico.[12] Although Cavelier may have located the Ohio River, there are no credible sources that detail where he ultimately traveled in 1669 and 1670.[13]

Cavelier's expeditions drew the attention of Canada Governor Louis de Buade, Comte de Frontenac et de Palluau (Frontenac), who in 1673, dispatched Cavelier to Onontagué, the capital of the Onondaga Iroquois to invite their leaders to a council. The governor hoped to negotiate with Iroquois headmen to obtain a small piece of Iroquois land located on the east end of Lake Ontario, at the mouth of the Cataraqui River. Deeply in debt, Frontenac had a personal interest in building a fort at that site. He could use the fort as an unobtrusive, yet illegal, trading post strategically located to intercept furs coming from the Upper Country, a fort that could provide him with continual income.[14] The Iroquois, who were preoccupied with other matters such as fighting wars with the Andaste and the Mohegan, unenthusiastically acquiesced to the governor's proposal. Without informing Minister Colbert of his intentions to build a post at the site, the governor ordered the

---

[10] Allouez had been called to quell the behavior of French traders at a Potawatomi village in Wisconsin. Kellogg, *Early Narratives*, 142.

[11] Francis Parkman, *La Salle and the Discovery of the Great West*, ed. Jon Krakauer (New York: Modern Library, 1999), 4-5.

[12] Talon to Colbert, October 10, 1670 and Colbert to Talon, November 2, 1671, both in "A Calendar of La Salle's Travels," *A Jean Delanglez Anthology*, ed. Mildred Mott Wedel (New York and London: Garland Publishing 1985), 283-285.

[13] The French administration in Canada in 1750 claimed that La Salle had discovered the Ohio River (in 1669). See "Memoir on the French Colonies in North America," in *Documents Relating to the Colonial History of New York*, ed. Edmund Bailey O'Callaghan, 15 volumes on CD (Saugerties, NY: Hope Farm Press, 2001), IX: 229. Hereafter cited as O'Callaghan, *DCHNY*.

[14] "Journal of Count de Frontenac's Voyage to Lake Ontario in 1673," O'Callaghan, *DCHNY*, IX: 95-114.

construction of Fort Frontenac.[15] Cavelier later sailed to France with letters of recommendation from the governor, written on Cavalier's behalf that petitioned for seigniorial rights over the property surrounding the fort and a patent of nobility.[16] Both petitions were granted. Cavelier had become a nobleman and could rightfully be called La Salle.

In late 1677, La Salle boarded a ship and sailed to France again, this time to petition French Minister of the Marine Jean-Baptiste Colbert for permission to "explore the gulf of Mexico by traversing the countries of North America."[17] Embedded in his request was a plan to exploit natural resources: bison hides, an increasingly valuable commodity, could be transported to a year-round, ice-free port on the Gulf via the rivers of the West with far less difficulty than carrying them through the Great Lakes and northern waterways to Montreal.[18] Moreover, should a rupture occur in the tenuous peace between the French and Iroquois and hostilities break out on the Great Lakes and St. Lawrence Valley, a port on the Gulf would ensure the uninterrupted flow of peltry to France. La Salle was no doubt confident that the king would approve his request since Colbert had suggested offering a royal award for the discovery in 1672.[19]

Through Colbert, the king granted La Salle a five-year patent that permitted him to "discover" the western part of New France to locate the road "to penetrate to Mexico." Although he was permitted to build forts wherever necessary, he was only allowed to trade in bison hides, and was strictly forbidden to acquire furs from the tribes whose peltry was destined for Montreal.[20]

Because La Salle was required to fund the entire venture himself, he immediately sought financial investors. Once secured, a portion of the capital was immediately used to employ carpenters, sawyers, blacksmiths, and other tradesmen from urban areas who were essential for building both ships and forts. La Salle

---

[15] W. J. Eccles, *The Canadian Frontier, 1534-1760*, revised ed. (Albuquerque: University of New Mexico Press, 2003), 107.

[16] O'Callaghan, *DCHNY*, IX: 122.

[17] Tonti in Kellogg, *Early Narratives*, 286.

[18] Melville B. Anderson (trans.), *Relations of the Discoveries and Voyages of Cavelier de La Salle from 1679 to 1681, The Official Narrative* (Chicago: Caxton Club, 1901), 15.

[19] Colbert to Talon, [February 11, 1671], RAPQ, 1931, 146. Wedel, *Delanglez Anthology*, 284-285 and "M. Colbert to M. Talon," in O'Callaghan, *DCHNY*, IX: 89.

[20] "Letters Patent, Granted by the King of France to the Sieur de La Salle, on the 12th May 1678," in *Historical Collections of Louisiana*, part I, ed. Benjamin Franklin French (New York: Wiley and Putnam, 1846), 35, 36.

Beaver was valuable for making hats, which were then fashionable in Europe. See Ann Carlos and Frank Lewis, "Fur Trade (1670-1870)," *EH.Net Encyclopedia*, ed. Robert Whaples (March 16, 2008). URL http://eh.net/encyclopedia/the-economic-history-of-the-fur-trade-1670-to-1870/. Last accessed July 17, 2019.

The Montreal merchants made their money off the beaver trade and the king did not want La Salle skimming the beaver hides destined for Montreal. Meanwhile, the bison trade was very new and only a consequence of French expansion into lands of bison hunting tribes. It was thought that bison hides would become a valuable commodity. This explains why La Salle chose Accault to be his trader to the bison-hunting trans-Mississippi tribes. Accault was probably the most experienced bison hide trader in New France at the time.

sought out military experience as well. Henri Tonti, who had served in the French military for eight years, became La Salle's most trusted deputy, playing an important role in the early French history of Illinois.[21] La Salle, Tonti, and more than thirty men sailed from France to Canada.

Arriving in Quebec in September 1678, La Salle sent men and matériel to rendezvous at Fort Frontenac, his base camp and embarkation point for the expedition. A few months later he sent carpenters to present-day Buffalo, New York, above Niagara Falls, to build a fort/storehouse enclosed by palisades, where his men and goods would be housed and his ship, the *Griffon*, would be built. The vessel's purpose was twofold: to transport men, weighty supplies, tools, and trade goods west through the Great Lakes and, until his port on the Gulf was erected, to haul heavy buffalo hides procured from the Indians, back to Canada. This ship was an essential component in the success of La Salle's enterprise.

Figure 3: A model of what La Salle's Griffon may have looked like.
Photo taken at the Lake Superior Maritime Visitor Center in Duluth, Minnesota by the author.

---

[21] Enrico Tonti (1650-1704) was Italian by birth but his family sought refuge in France and his father Gallicized their names and added the dignified yet fictional "de." Henri joined the French army and lost his right hand, which was replaced with an artificial one. His name was later Anglicized to "Tonty." Background information can be found at: https://www.findagrave.com/memorial/128400498/henri-de_tonti.

Ahead of his expedition, La Salle also dispatched a group of men west, first to the Mississippi Valley to trade for bison hides.[22] After procuring the hides, the men were instructed to deliver them to an island on Green Bay for transport east on La Salle's ship. Leading this group was Michel Accault, who had experienced trading with trans-Mississippi buffalo hunting tribes such as the Iowa, Otoe, and Little Prairie Sioux located in today's northern Missouri and Iowa, and possibly as far north as southern Minnesota.[23] Accault reportedly had a "slight acquaintance" with their languages," such as Chiwere, and knew many of their "ways."[24] He also knew the location of their villages including that of the "Otontanta," or the Otoe Indians, as illustrated on Marquette's 1673 map along today's Des Moines River. Accault's group was also instructed to go "among the Illinois," likely to the Peoria villages that Jolliet and Marquette had visited during their voyage that were located some distance downstream from the Otoe village.[25] Unlike other French traders during this time, Accault knew the bison business. He was La Salle's representative, negotiator, and point man in the bison trade, someone who the explorer hoped could integrate the individual tribes, from different regions, into one intertribal trade network.

Leaving Niagara, the ship's first stop was at Michilimackinac, at the nexus of Lakes Michigan and Huron, where La Salle learned that most of Accault's party had deserted, taking the majority of the trade goods and supplies with them.[26] Several deserters including Gabriel Minime le Barbier, a fugitive, who La Salle would later pardon and reintegrate into his group.[27] Learning that two other deserters had fled to the French post at Sault Ste. Marie, the explorer directed Tonti and six men to find and arrest them and to seize the stolen goods. His assignment completed, Tonti was instructed by La Salle to rendezvous with him at the mouth of the St. Joseph River.

Leaving Michilimackinac, the *Griffon* sailed to one of the Door County peninsula islands where Accault waited with a large quantity of buffalo hides worth more than "twelve thousand livres." The bundles loaded onto the ship, La Salle gave

---

[22] The exact number of men in the party is unknown. According to *La Salle's Relation*, "Upon Landing at Michilimackinac, M. de La Salle was greatly surprised to find here the majority of the men he had sent on in advance, to the number of fifteen, having supposed them to be long since among the Illinois." It is uncertain if La Salle sent fifteen men in advance, or if fifteen men deserted from the advanced party. Anderson, *Relation of La Salle*, 41.

[23] Accault had previously traded for La Salle out of his seigniory at Fort Frontenac. Mildred Mott Wedel, "Peering at the Ioway Indians Through the Mist of Time; 1650 circa 1700," *The Journal of the Iowa Archaeological Society* vol. 33 (1986): 30-32.

[24] Margry, *Découvertes*, II: 245. How much Chiwere Accault knew is unclear. La Salle wrote in one document that Accault had a "slight acquaintance" with the language but also wrote that he was "sufficiently versed" in it. Anderson, *Relation of La Salle*, 117.

[25] Ibid., 41. Marquette recorded that there were two Peoria villages at the site. Marquette in Thwaites, *Jesuit Relations*, LIX: 117.

[26] La Salle arrested four of worst offenders and sent Tonti to Sault Sainte Marie to find the others. Anderson, *Relation of La Salle*, 41, 43, 45.

[27] Gabriel Minime le Barbier would accompany the explorer to the Gulf in 1682 and to Texas in 1684. He would father the first *known* child of European parents born in today's Texas.

the captain specific instructions: deliver the cargo to Niagara, load up the tools and equipment waiting there, and return to Michilimackinac to await further orders. Having instructed the captain, La Salle and his remaining men journeyed in canoes down the western shore of Lake Michigan. They passed the mouth of the Chicago River and paddled the coastline of today's Indiana and southern Michigan, landing at the mouth of the St. Joseph River. There, La Salle's men began constructing a small post called Fort Miami.

It seems strange that La Salle chose to pass the mouth of the Chicago River, the well-known route to the Illinois, and chose instead to paddle an additional ninety-seven miles to the St. Joseph. A likely explanation for establishing himself there is that the explorer hoped to entice the Miami of the region to join his coalition of tribes. It is possible too, that La Salle wanted to avoid the half-league portage located between the Chicago and Des Plaines Rivers, a known significant navigational impediment, choosing instead to portage to the Kankakee River via the St. Joseph.[28]

In late November, Tonti, his men, and the captured deserters arrived at the St. Joseph fort. Tonti informed La Salle that he had not seen the *Griffon*, nor had he heard any news of it, even though the vessel should have long since arrived at Michilimackinac.[29] La Salle sent two men back north to determine what had become of his missing ship. In the meantime, La Salle and his crew departed for Kaskaskia. Despite the serious financial complication that the potential loss of the *Griffon* presented, La Salle had, nonetheless, to travel to Illinois before the onset of winter curtailed river navigation.

Paddling up the St. Joseph, La Salle and his thirty-three-man entourage disembarked somewhere near present-day South Bend, Indiana where he began the muddy trek through the marsh toward the headwaters of the Kankakee River. Sometime during the march, a disgruntled Frenchman named Duplessis shouldered his arquebus, intending to shoot La Salle from behind. The attempt on La Salle's life was somehow thwarted by another member of the party.[30] The French eventually reached the Kankakee and continued their journey downriver. Becoming

---

[28] We will see in chapter two that Jolliet had reported the difficult Chicago to Des Plaines River portage to Claude Dablon, Jesuit Superior of Canada in 1674.

Two types of leagues were used by the French during the seventeenth-century including the *lieue ancienne* and the *lieue de Paris*. Besides their different lengths, the measurement of the *lieue ancienne*, for example, could vary in different parts of France. It could also change if used for nautical or surface measurements. Historians such as Joseph Zitomersky and Marcel Trudel have approximated a seventeenth-century league to be about three miles. Considering the problems associated with determining league lengths, the imprecise approximations of distances traveled on winding rivers, and other factors, we have not endeavored to accurately calculate the distances of the leagues used by La Salle. We left the word "league" as it appears in the sources. See Joseph Zitomersky, *French Americans: Native Americans in Eighteenth Century French Colonial Louisiana* (Lund, Sweden: Lund University Press, 1995), XXIII.

[29] Several individuals claim to have found the missing ship. See, for example, http:// greatlakesexploration .org/expedition.htm.

[30] *Relation of Henri de Tonty Concerning the Explorations of La Salle from 1678 to 1683*, trans. Melville B. Anderson (Chicago: Caxton Club, 1898), 27.

increasingly exasperated with the hardships and difficulties of travel in the wilderness, La Salle's men began to realize not only the depth of their predicament, but the limited recourse that they had to remedy the discomfort. In a hostile and alien expanse of land that extended in every direction, one where a simple accident or an Indian ambush could cost them their lives, fear was omnipresent. Travel was slow while tempers likely flared. Hunger became a major concern as the prairies that oft provided plentiful game lay burned and lifeless, after the local Indians set them ablaze during their hunts. Cold, without refuge or convenience, two thirds of La Salle's men had by mid-December conspired to desert at night, hoping to take the canoes and anything they could haul in them. This plot, like the one to murder La Salle at the portage, was likewise foiled. The crew understood that only after they reached Kaskaskia would they find food and shelter.

CHAPTER TWO
RAPIDS, FORTS, AND BARKS

It was late December when La Salle's canoes reached the Forks, the confluence of the Kankakee and Des Plaines Rivers that merge to form the Illinois. Descending the Illinois, the French passed through "the most beautiful country in the world," as La Salle described them, lands "intersected by streams and diversified with meadows, islands, clumps of trees, hills, valleys and plains where the land is excellent and, best of all, the river." After having traveled about 29 miles, the party encountered a set of rapids located along a stretch of river at today's Marseilles, Illinois. La Salle was likely quite surprised to have encountered the sault, a riverine feature that he later wrote made navigation along this stretch of river, "very difficult," even when "the waters are high."[1]

Figure 4: Illinois River Rapids at Marseilles, Illinois.
About these rapids, Frenchman Henri Joutel wrote: "the bottom of the river was full of rocks and stones which were very uncomfortable, and notably for me." Photo by the author.

Three months later, these same rapids, a prominent geological feature, would become a reference point in the vast western wilderness where La Salle would

---

[1] Letters of Cavelier de La Salle and Correspondence Relative to his Undertakings (1678-1685)," *Miami Tribal History Document Series, Great Lakes - Ohio Valley Ethnohistory Collection, Erminie Wheeler-Voegelin Archives*, Indiana University, Bloomington.

rendezvous with several of his men during the explorer's long winter trek from the Illinois Country to Fort Frontenac.[2] So turbulent was this sault that Henri Joutel, a Frenchman who encountered these same rapids in 1688 during his journey from Starved Rock to Quebec wrote,

> I can say that I had more trouble and pain doing this [negotiating the Marseilles rapids] than during the entire trip, for, to start with, at that place where the rapid was, the bottom of the river was full of rocks and stones which were very uncomfortable, and notably for me.[3]

In order to understand why La Salle was surprised and likely troubled when he encountered these rapids, we must examine the substance of a meeting held at Quebec between Louis Jolliet and Claude Dablon, Jesuit Superior of Canada. Further, we need to understand how two maps drawn by Jean-Baptiste Franquelin for Jolliet influenced La Salle's understanding of the course of the Illinois River.

Returning from the Mississippi River expedition, Jolliet spent the winter of 1673-1674 at his trade post at Sault Ste. Marie. After ice-out, he left the Sault and headed to Quebec with two men and a young Indian boy in a canoe that also carried Marquette's journal and likely an assortment of items that the explorers had collected during their expedition. At a rapid in the St. Lawrence River within sight of Montreal, disaster struck. The canoe capsized and everyone and everything aboard—the men, the boy, Marquette's journal, and the items collected—were lost. Only Jolliet survived the wreck.[4]

It took approximately nine months before a copy of Marquette's journal, a detailed report that included an accurate map of his and Jolliet's journey, reached Quebec. Until then, Canadian authorities would have to rely on Jolliet's testimony to learn what the two explorers had encountered during their travels. On August 1, 1674 Jolliet met with Dablon, the essence of their meeting, as it applies to discoveries in the Illinois Country, is recorded in *Jesuit Relations*, volume 58.[5]

About the Illinois Country, Jolliet reported to Dablon, "At first, when we were told of these treeless lands [by the Indians], I imagined that it was a country ravaged by fire, where the soil was so poor that it could produce nothing." "But," he continued, "we have certainly observed the contrary; and no better soil can be found, either for corn, for vines, or for any other fruit whatever." Jolliet also told Dablon that "A settler would not there spend ten years in cutting down and burning the trees; on the very day of his arrival, he could put his plow into the ground."[6] In

---

[2] *Relations of the Discoveries and Voyages of Cavelier de La Salle from 1679 to 1681, The Official Narrative,* trans. Melville B. Anderson (Chicago: Caxton Club, 1901), 155.
[3] Margry, *Découvertes*, III: 508. Translation by Michael McCafferty, Indiana University, Bloomington.
[4] Thwaites, *Jesuit Relations*, LVIII: 105.
[5] Jolliet, a good Catholic and friend of the Jesuits, met with Dablon to give him a verbal account of his and Marquette's journey. Marquette's annual report, one that was required by Jesuit policy, had been lost during Jolliet's canoe wreck. This likely explains why Jolliet met with Dablon shortly after his arrival in Quebec.
[6] Thwaites, *Jesuit Relations*, LVIII: 105.

addition, Jolliet reported that "Game is abundant there; oxen [buffalo], cows, stags, does, and Turkeys are found there in greater numbers than elsewhere."[7]

Besides describing the fertile lands and the variety and abundance of game in the Illinois Country, Jolliet reported that a bark, a large commercial sailing vessel, could sail from Lake Erie to Florida, "by *easy* navigation," something that Dablon wrote was a "very great and important advantage, which perhaps will hardly be believed." The only obstacle along this route lay at the marshy stretch of land located between the Chicago and Des Plaines Rivers where, according to Jolliet, it would be necessary to dig a canal a half-league in length to connect the two streams. Dablon recorded the route that the bark would take:

> [It] would be built on lake Erie, which is near Lake Ontario, it would easily pass from lake Erie to lake Huron, whence it would enter lake Illinois. At the end of that lake the canal or excavation of which I have spoken would be made, to gain a passage into the river Saint Louis, which falls into the Mississipi. The bark, when there, would easily sail to the gulf of Mexico.[8]

Furthermore, Jolliet described the Illinois River as "wide and deep, abounding in catfish and sturgeon," indicating that the stream was deep enough to enable large vessels to sail its course. Except for the stretch of land at the Chicago portage, Jolliet reported no other navigational impediments between today's Buffalo, New York, and the Gulf of Mexico.

Canada governor Frontenac enthusiastically relayed Jolliet's report to French Minister Colbert. However, the governor wrote that the only impasse between La Salle's Fort Frontenac and the Gulf was not at the Chicago portage, but at Niagara Falls. According to Frontenac:

> [Jolliet] has returned three months ago, and discovered some very fine Countries, and a navigation so easy through the beautiful rivers he has found, that a person can go from Lake Ontario and Fort Frontenac in a bark to the Gulf of Mexico, there being only one carrying place, half a league in length, where Lake Ontario communicates with Lake Erie. A settlement could be made at this point and another bark built on Lake Erie.[9]

Continuing, Frontenac reported that Jolliet had traveled "within ten days' journey of the Gulf of Mexico, and believes that water communications could be found leading to the Vermilion and California seas, by means of the river [likely the Missouri River] that flows from the West into the Grand River that he discovered, which runs from North to South, and is as large as the Saint Lawrence opposite Quebec."

Sometime after meeting with the Jesuit Superior, Jolliet collaborated with Jean-Baptiste Franquelin, a skilled calligrapher—not a cartographer—at this time,

---

[7] Ibid.
[8] Ibid., 103. Emphasis added.
[9] O'Callaghan, *DCHNY*, IX: 121.

to draw two maps of the route of the 1673 voyage.[10] Having lost Marquette's precise map and journal in the canoe wreck, documents that recorded latitude readings, names of Indian tribes that the explorers encountered, and the locations of rivers and lakes with their associated portages, Jolliet had to provide information about the route and discoveries from memory.

Franquelin's first map was the 1674 *La Colbertie*, a chart that dedicated the "newly discovered" western lands and the Mississippi River in honor of French Minister Colbert. The following year Franquelin completed his second map, one known as *La Frontenacie* as it names the western lands after Canada governor Frontenac, and the Mississippi in honor of Frontenac's family name, Buade. Both *La Colbertie* and *La Frontenacie* maps were, according to Canadian historian Lucien Campeau, petitions to French officials for "payment and a gratuity" for services rendered to the colonial and French governments.[11] Drawn without the benefit of detailed cartographical information, the two maps were less than accurate by today's standards.

More specifically, the 1675 Jolliet-Franquelin map illustrates the names of tribes and locations of Indian villages in the Mississippi Valley. One tribe, the Mosopelea, was depicted as living on the east side of the Mississippi River below the mouth of the Arkansas River. Furthermore, the map shows "Europeans" living near the Gulf in of today's states of Louisiana and Mississippi. The Mosopelea and the presence of Europeans near the Gulf on the map will become points of contention that will be discussed later in this narrative.[12]

With his two maps intended to influence Canada's governor and a French minister, Jolliet petitioned Colbert through Canada's Intendant Jacques Duchesneau for permission to establish a colony with 20 men in the Illinois Country. Jolliet's selling points to Colbert were surely the suitability of Illinois lands for settlement and the potential for French trade and commerce via the newly discovered western waterways.[13]

---

[10] Lucien Campeau, "The Maps Relative to the Discovery of the Missisipi [sic] by Father Jacques Marquette and Louis Jolliet," in *Les Cahiers des Dix,* trans. Michael McCafferty (Bloomington, IN, 2004), 60. Franquelin came to Canada from France in 1671 to engage in the colony's fur trade. It is possible that he learned the rudiments of mapmaking as a boy in France. See M.W. Burke-Gaffney, Franquelin, Jean-Baptiste-Louis," in *Dictionary of Canadian Biography* (Toronto: University of Toronto Press, 1969, revised 2003), II: 228.

[11] Campeau, "Maps," 63, 71.

[12] According to Campeau, the only reason why the names of Indian tribes were noted on the 1675 Jolliet-Franquelin map and not on the 1674 map is because it was not until about May of 1675 that Marquette's relation and map arrived in Quebec.

[13] "Extraite d' une lettre de Colbert à M. Du Chesneau" in Margry, *Découvertes,* I: 329 and Jean Delanglez S.J., *Life and Voyages of Louis Jolliet, 1645-1700* (Chicago: Institute of Jesuit History, 1948), 135-136.

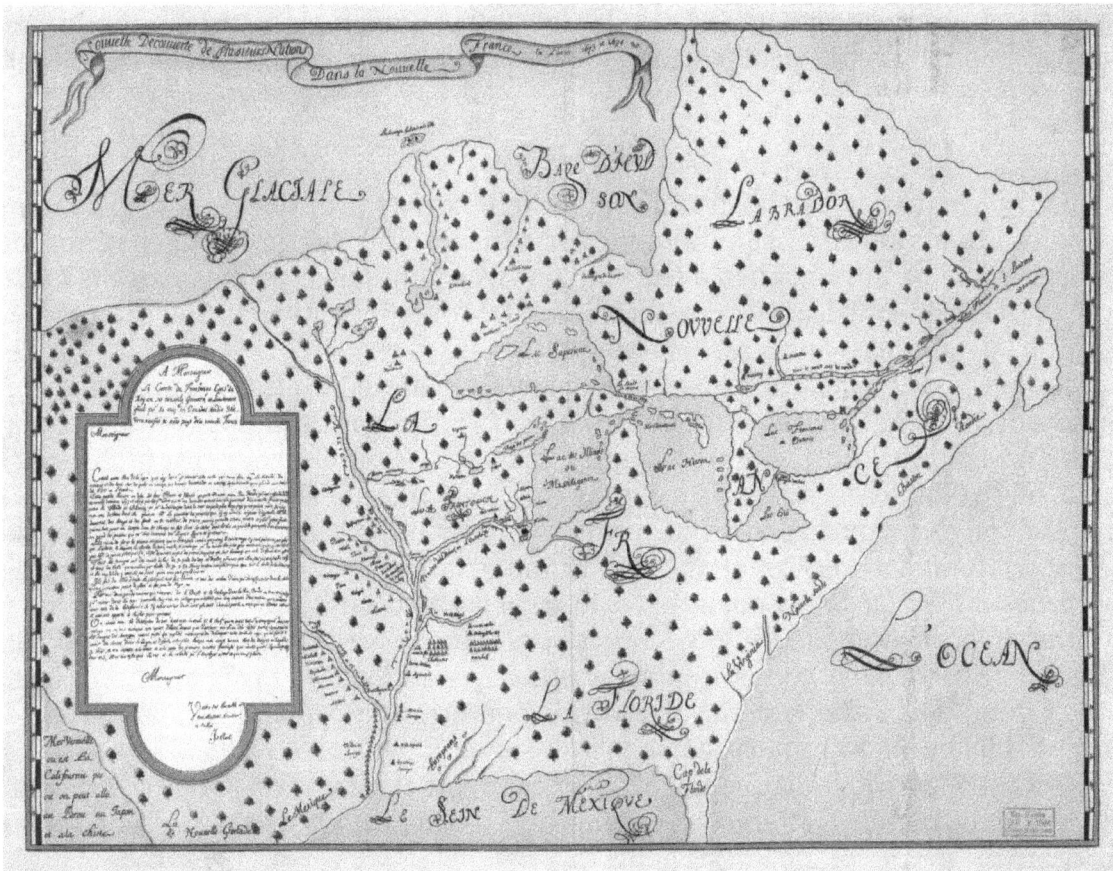

Figure 5: Image of Franquelin's 1675 map,
also known as *La Frontenacie*, based on information provided by Louis Jolliet.
Map courtesy of the Library of Congress. https://www.loc.gov/resource/g3300.ct000655/.

Colbert denied Jolliet's request to settle in the distant Illinois Country, preferring instead to concentrate Canada's population along the lower St. Lawrence River, rather than to spread Frenchmen thinly across the Great Lakes and into the Mississippi Valley. Although this was Colbert's official reason for denying Jolliet's request to settle in the West, an underlying reason may have been Jolliet's close relationship and association with the Jesuits, a powerful Catholic religious order whose ambitions often conflicted with those of secular authorities. The historical record reveals that Jolliet had attended the Jesuit college in Quebec, intending to one day enter the priesthood. He was a musician who had played the organ in the cathedral of Quebec "for many years."[14] He was a friend of Bishop Laval, the powerful church official who had lent him money to travel to France in 1667. And it was with Dablon, Jesuit Superior of Canada, whom Jolliet first met with upon his return to Quebec. Jolliet's earlier association with church officials, specifically the Jesuits, was likely too close for the comfort of secular authorities, and it may have

---

[14] André Vachon, "Louis Jolliet," *Dictionary of Canadian Biography*, vol. I, 1000-1700 (Toronto: University of Toronto Press, 1979), 392-393.

been one untold reason why Colbert denied Jolliet's request to settle in the Illinois Country.[15] But Colbert's plan to keep Canada's population huddled in the East would soon change.

––––––––––––

For La Salle's plan to establish working trade relations with the western tribes and transport their hides to ships bound for France, and subsequently pay for his enterprise, he had to establish a working line of communication between the Lakes and the Gulf of Mexico *via* the Illinois and Mississippi Rivers. Since La Salle's petition to Colbert included making "the discovery of the mouth [of the Mississippi]," the explorer must have sincerely believed Jolliet's report that one could sail from the Chicago Portage to the Gulf of Mexico without encountering any major navigational obstacles, making the transportation of heavy bison hides to a port on the Gulf easier than the arduous trek to Montreal. After all, had Jolliet not told Dablon that one could sail this route by "easy navigation," something that the Jesuit wrote was a "very great and important advantage, which perhaps will hardly be believed?"[16] La Salle must have also believed that Franquelin's two maps accurately portrayed the Illinois River as an obstacle-free highway that led to the Mississippi since he noted no rapids or other navigational hazards on them. In La Salle's mind all the components of a working enterprise were in place: large villages occupied by buffalo-hunting people who lived on a navigable waterway that led to the Gulf. Armed with what he believed was reliable information about the western lands and the region's waterways, La Salle and the men of his first expedition set out to locate the mouth of the Mississippi.

La Salle's party likely portaged around the rapids at Marseilles and then continued their trek downstream. It was New Year's Day 1680 when La Salle's eight canoes passed the mouth of the Fox River and, an hour later, Buffalo Rock, the future site of the state park of the same name. Passing Buffalo Rock, La Salle's canoe men saw that the river had again become shallow and rocky. But the French canoes kept moving, navigating the channel between the large island known on late 19th and early 20th-century maps as Delbridge or Goose Island, and the river's north bank. Approaching Kaskaskia, La Salle's men saw no signs of life, no barking dogs to alert the Indians of intruders, no smoke issuing from the cabins, and no inquisitive Indians at the shore to receive the approaching Frenchmen. What La Salle knew, and likely kept from his hungry and disgruntled men, was that the Illinois were gone, having relocated to winter hunting camps farther downstream. The French canoes landed on the upstream end of a mile-long portage located at east end of the village.[17] Immediately La Salle's men left their canoes and began surveying the village, hoping to find something to eat. Likely after they had rifled through the Indian huts and scoured the grounds, they located the Indian's buried maize, *miinčipi* in the Miami-

––––––––––––

[15] Ibid.
[16] Weddle, Morkovsky, and Galloway, *Minet Relation*, 31 and Thwaites, *Jesuit Relations*, LVIII: 105.
[17] Marquette wrote that Kaskaskia was located at a portage one-half league in length. *Jesuit Relations* LIX: 159.

Illinois language, a cache that, according to La Salle, had been previously discovered by other Indians who had passed the village.[18] Disregarding its ownership, the crew appropriated about forty bushels of the grain for themselves. La Salle knew that taking any amount of this precious commodity was a serious offense. The Indians had set aside this maize so that it would provide the village with food in the spring and would serve as seed for the next season's crop. Any shortage could cause the Indians to go hungry. But realizing that his men were hungry and that there was little hope of locating game along their route since the Illinois Country prairies had been burned by the Indians, La Salle had little choice but to take the maize. He hoped to cover this theft by later giving the Indians gifts.

While the men loaded maize into their canoes, Father Zenobe Membré, a Recollet missionary attached to La Salle's expedition, walked through the deserted village, counting the Indian structures. When he finished his survey, the priest noted that there were 460 huts.[19] Kaskaskia's population had grown considerably larger than it had been when Allouez had ministered to the Indians at the village in 1677, having increased by over 100 cabins.

Figure 6: Site of the Grand Village of the Illinois, also known as Kaskaskia by the French and *kaaskaaskinki* or *kaaskaaskingi* by the Illinois who lived at the site. Photo by the author.

With his men rested and likely fed, La Salle determined to locate the Indians rather than wait for them to return to the village. The group boarded their canoes and continued downriver. Unsure about what lay ahead, the flotilla proceeded slowly. For the next several miles the group paddled their canoes through the

---

[18] "Letter from La Salle to One of his Partners," Margry, *Découvertes*, II: 37. It seems strange that La Salle did not mention to the Illinois at Lake Peoria that other Indians, people who he labeled as enemies of the Illinois, had also taken some of the maize. *Miinčipi* is the general term for maize in the Miami-Illinois language. Michael McCafferty, "Illinois Voices, Observations on the Miami-Illinois Language," in Robert F. Mazrim, *Protohistory of the Grand Village of the Kaskaskia, The Illinois Country on the Eve of Colony*, Studies in Archaeology no. 10 (Urbana: Illinois State Archaeological Survey, 2015), 127.

[19] Anderson, *Relation La Salle*, 85. Four hundred and sixty residential "cabins" would represent a population of over 9,000.

shallow water and between the islands and small "rapids," as later cartographers would call them. Passing tall sandstone cliffs including Starved Rock, Lover's Leap, and Eagle Cliff, the party eventually found deeper water near the mouth of today's Vermilion River. Along their journey, the French flotilla passed today's "Clam Beds," "Big Bend," "Twin Sister Islands," and the wide floodplain that would become Lake Senachwine. Somewhere along this stretch of river the group lucked upon a herd of buffalo crossing the river in mid-stream. Taking advantage of the opportunity to procure a supply of meat, La Salle's men killed and butchered several of them. Four days after leaving Kaskaskia, the French reached a broad expanse of the river, today's Lake Peoria. Near sunset, they observed smoke rising from a pair of Indian camps some distance ahead. Rather than approach the Indians late in the day, La Salle decided to wait until morning.

The next morning, the French cautiously paddled toward the camps, one of which La Salle reported was "swarming with Indians" with a few *mihsoori*, wooden dugout canoes, beached along each river bank. This was a winter encampment of Illinois Indians, a site consisting of about eighty cabins.[20] Floating with the current in single file, La Salle's party managed to slip within "half a gunshot" range of one of the camps. To announce his presence, La Salle stood in the canoe and shouted, so that the Indians would hear him.[21] Immediately, alarm spread throughout the village. Uncertain if La Salle was friend or foe, panicked women and children ran to the safety of the concealing timber, while Indian men seized their weapons and prepared to fight. In the confusion, La Salle leapt ashore ahead of his men, but halted "to restore confidence to the Indians." Hoping to avoid bloodshed, village chiefs held up smoking pipes called calumets, gestures La Salle immediately recognized and accepted.

After initial greetings had been exchanged, La Salle addressed the village chiefs at a council. Having offered their hosts gifts of good will, La Salle immediately addressed the matter of the pilfered maize. La Salle offered to return the maize to the Illinois if they wanted it, or, alternatively, offered payment to settle the matter. To pressure the Illinois to accept the offer, La Salle told them that if they forbade his men to keep the maize, he would continue his journey downstream and buy maize from the Osage Indians. In that bargain, La Salle explained that he would, in addition, give the tribe hatchets and other goods and assign a blacksmith to remain at their villages.[22] Knowing the importance of establishing commercial ties with the French, the Illinois accepted La Salle's offer of payment and the matter was resolved. La Salle also told the Illinois that he planned to "bring other Frenchmen, who would secure them from the insults of their enemies, the Iroquois, and would furnish them with everything they required."[23] The Indians welcomed this news as they had lived under constant threat of Iroquois attack for many years. Equally important was the

---

[20] Eighty Illinois cabins equals about approximately 1,600 village inhabitants. The formula used to calculate approximate village population is explained in chapter six.

[21] Ibid., 87, 89.

[22] Ibid., 91-93.

[23] Ibid., 95.

offer of trade goods. The Indians accepted all of La Salle's "proposals" and offered him their help, if it were needed.

The bargain was struck. During the night, however, a Miami chief named "Moonswa" arrived at the Illinois camp with a message from their trusted and respected missionary, Father Allouez. Moonswa, the Deer, a name that would evolve into Monseau or Monso, told the Illinois not to trust La Salle—that he was "a brother to the Iroquois," and that he breathed Iroquois breath.[24] Moonswa told the Illinois that La Salle was planning to arm the Mississippi tribes to their west, as well as their Iroquois enemies to the east, essentially pinning the Illinois between the two powerful and well-armed adversaries. He told the Illinois that La Salle was "abhorred" by their black-robed friends, the Jesuits, who considered him to be an Iroquois. So treacherous was La Salle, Moonswa told the tribesmen, that he even possessed a powerful potion that could poison everyone in their village.[25] As tokens of his sincerity, Moonswa gave the Illinois obligatory gifts, kettles, hatchets, and knives, items that were from Allouez himself. With his message delivered, the Miami and his companions disappeared into the snowy night and headed back to their Wisconsin village. Moonswa's late-night visit would not remain a secret among the Indians for long, as Omoahoha, an Illinois chief who La Salle had befriended the day before, told him everything that had transpired. Until there was opportunity to clear his name to the Illinois chiefs, La Salle would keep the information to himself.

Sometime during the next afternoon, the Illinois chiefs and elders gathered for a feast, an event to which La Salle and his men were summoned. With everyone seated, a principal chief named Nicanapé stood and addressed La Salle personally, beseeching him to not descend the Mississippi, hoping to "cure him" of his disease of going there. The chief told the explorer that no one can run the Mississippi gauntlet and survive. Many fierce, warlike tribes lived along its banks, whose warriors pounce on unsuspecting travelers. "Monsters and serpents" also lived just beneath the river's surface, and if those hazards weren't enough, rapids, violent torrents, and cascades in the lower parts of the river pull canoes into an underground gulf and into ultimate oblivion. Nicanapé's tone was serious and his pleadings emotional and they caught the attention of La Salle's men.

La Salle sat unmoved, patiently waiting for Nicanapé to finish his speech, yet impatient to challenge Moonswa's false allegations. He knew that the Indians would consider it both rude and offensive to interrupt the chief while he was speaking. When the latter had finally finished his cautionary discourse, La Salle stood and calmly and deliberately addressed the Illinois headmen. He thanked Nicanapé for warning him about the monsters and hazards on the Mississippi but told the chief that "the greater the obstacles to be surmounted the greater the glory they would gain." He informed the chief that he served "the greatest of all captains" and was "happy to die bearing the king's name to the ends of the earth." La Salle also told them that he was well-aware that Nicanapé's warning, his "friendly fiction," was

---

[24] Pease and Werner, *French Foundations,* 12-13. Michael McCaffery, personal correspondence, February 21, 2013.
[25] Ibid. 12-13.

intended to discourage him from trading with more distant tribes that would deprive the Illinois of their trade advantage. He told the Illinois that if the French and Illinois were friends, as the Illinois had led him to believe, then he, La Salle, would explain his actions to them, the Illinois.

The explorer next addressed the more important issue at hand, that of Moonswa and his late-night visit to the Illinois camp. Speaking to Nicanapé personally, La Salle told the chief that he was surprised that Nicanapé actually believed the Miami's lies. He also told the chief that he knew that Moonswa's bribes were buried under the very lodge in which they were sitting. Why, La Salle asked, did Moonswa come in secret at night and not during the day? And why did he steal away into the darkness immediately after telling his lies? La Salle reminded the chief that he could have killed Nicanapé and his people when he first arrived at the village since most of the warriors were away hunting, and he could kill everyone now if he chose to do so. La Salle asked the chief how Moonswa could possibly know that La Salle had consorted with the Iroquois when the Miami had never been among the Iroquois nor had met La Salle? La Salle further challenged Nicanapé to search the French canoes in order to verify that they carried only tools and trade goods, and not weapons.

La Salle's scolding resonated with the Indians, so much so that they considered taking up the chase to track down and kill Moonswa. Fortunately for the Miami, heavy snowfall during the night obscured his tracks, making pursuit difficult if not impossible.[26]

It was predictable and reasonable for La Salle's men to question whether to remain with him in a situation that was bound in misfortune or risk striking out on their own in hopes of encountering friendly *coureur de bois*, taking refuge with them, and eventually returning to France. One enterprising crew member, however, chose a third option: he attempted to poison La Salle. The would-be murderer was unsuccessful, as La Salle is said to have carried an antidote that saved his life.[27]

Considering the circumstances in which La Salle now found himself, he determined that his best course of action would be to leave the Illinois camp and set up his winter quarters elsewhere, not too close, yet not too far from the Illinois. The move facilitated ongoing contact and friendship with the Illinois while still providing distance for security. The French left the village and settled about a mile and a half downstream, on the opposite shore of the river. There, the men began construction of Fort de Crèvecoeur, a wooden fortification surrounded by ravines, a trench, and a marsh. There, and not farther upstream, because of the geology of the Illinois River, La Salle's carpenters also began building a new sailing vessel, a forty-ton bark, forty-two feet long by twelve feet wide to transport supplies, materiel, and men to the Gulf to build the fort. The bark would later be used to haul bison hides between Crèvecoeur and the Gulf.

Today, we know that the Illinois River is actually two rivers; the westerly flowing portion of the stream that flows between the Forks and the Big Bend, the

---

[26] Anderson, *Relation of La Salle*, 107.
[27] "Memoir of the Sieur de La Tonty," in *Historical Collections of Louisiana*, I: 54.

ninety-degree curve in the river just north of today's Hennepin, Illinois, and the southern-southwesterly flowing portion of the river between the Big Bend and its confluence with the Mississippi River. The Illinois River above the Big Bend is a new stream, probably no more than about 14,000 years old. This part of the Illinois River Valley was carved from the landscape by torrents of glacial melt water at the close of the last Ice Age. Attesting to the young age of the upper Illinois River are geological features such as rapids and scattered boulders and shoals.[28] In fact, the portion of the Illinois River that flows through La Salle County has the steepest declivity and swiftest current of any part of the river. Furthermore, white pine and white cedar, trees that typically grow in northern environs such as Wisconsin, Michigan, and across eastern Canada, sprout from sheer sandstone cliffs and assorted rock formations that border the river at places such as today's Starved Rock State Park. Below the Big Bend, however, the river is a slow-moving stream, one so lethargic that at the point where the river encounters a small alluvial deposit composed of sand emanating from the mouth of Sandy Creek, located in Marshall County, the Illinois River, instead of pushing the debris away, it curves around it. This portion of the Illinois is the ancient Mississippi River, millions of years old, where wide flood plains and large backwater swamps, such as the one at Emiquon in Fulton County, Illinois are found.[29] The two distinct types of landscapes along the two Illinois Rivers are obvious to an interested observer. It is logical to assume that La Salle, an explorer who recorded a host of important and seemingly insignificant observations during his journeys saw the differences between the rocky and rapid strewn Illinois River that tumbled below tall cliffs, where trees typical of northern regions grew, and those of the broad, slow-moving river that flowed through wide and flat floodplains below the Big Bend. By the time La Salle reached Lake Peoria, the explorer likely believed that his group had long passed the rapids and shallow stretches of the upper Illinois River and were on deeper and more navigable water.

Further reinforcing La Salle's belief that the river was now navigable below Fort Crèvecoeur was a map drawn by an Indian with whom the explorer had a chance encounter while hunting near the fort. According to La Salle,

> With a bit of charcoal the young man drew upon a sheet of bark a very accurate map, stating that he had been everywhere in his pirogue [dugout canoe], that one could reach the sea without encountering either falls or rapids, but that, where the river became very wide, there were occasional sand bars and mud banks, which would choke some part of the channel.[30]

---

[28] In a geological sense, the swift current of the upper Illinois has not had enough time to erode the river's rapids and reduce the boulders to powder.

[29] Raymond Wiggers, *Geology Underfoot in Illinois* (Missoula, MT: Mountain Press Company, 1997), 141-142.

[30] Anderson, *Relation of La Salle*, 139. Hennepin also references this chance meeting with the Illinois and the charcoal map, Louis Hennepin, *A New Discovery of a Vast Country in America*, ed. Reuben Gold Thwaites, 2 vols. (Toronto: Coles Publishing, 1903), I: 175.

Figure 7: Sheer St. Peter Sandstone cliffs covered with eastern white pine and cedar are typical of the Starved Rock area. Photo by the author.

A day or two later, a group of Osage, Chickasaw, and Arkansas Indians appeared at the fort to trade for a few hatchets. These tribesmen, like the Indian that the explorer had met in the forest, told La Salle that the Illinois and Mississippi Rivers were navigable "to the sea," all the way to the Gulf. They also told him that news of the arrival of the French has been announced "everywhere," and that the French, would be welcomed at the villages of these tribes. This new information, provided by people who lived on and had actually navigated the Illinois and Mississippi Rivers, combined with the explorer's personal observations would have given La Salle confidence that he had passed beyond the navigational hazards of the Illinois River. This conviction that his bark could sail uninterrupted to the sea, prompted La Salle, later that year to write to Frontenac that "It is possible to go by water from Fort Crevècoeur to the sea."[31]

In mid-February, while the French were busy felling trees for palisades, and sawing logs into planks for living quarters, a job made more difficult by the desertion of his sawyers, La Salle received a delegation of Otoe Indians.[32] Their arrival required the Otoe to travel deep into Illinois territory, which indicates the significant size and scope of the trade network that the explorer had begun to establish.

[31] Pease and Werner, *French Foundations*, 4.

[32] Ibid. The Otoe were a buffalo hunting tribe. La Salle's men deserted from the expedition making it necessary for the explorer to train new sawyers. See Anderson, *Relation of La Salle*, 183.

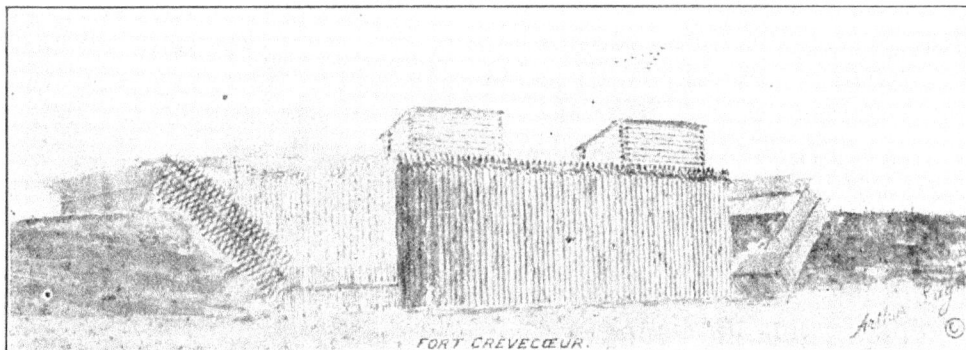

A REPRESENTATION OF THE OLD FRENCH FORT NEAR PEORIA

Figure 8: La Salle's Fort de Crèvecoeur. Photo courtesy Illinois State Historical Society.

It is likely that Accault's activities created both the knowledge and the impetus for the Otoe visit. La Salle's trader, Accault had traded for bison hides with the trans-Mississippi River tribes including the Otoe and, having been among the tribe in 1679, he would have informed them that La Salle would be arriving in the Illinois Country by 1680. It is logical that the Otoe delegation to Crèvecoeur sought to ensure that their relations and their trade ties with the French remained intact. European trade goods, to the tribes at the far fringe of French influence, like the Otoe, meant more than simply obtaining items that improved their quality of life, enhanced their appearance, or made them more proficient in war. These items were also a source of power and influence over tribes who lived beyond the range of European trade, who were not yet able to acquire these items directly from the French. The goods made the Otoe middlemen between the French and the more distant tribes. The seemingly insignificant appearance of the Otoe at Crèvecoeur provides insight to the extent to which La Salle's trading sphere influence had spread. The explorer hoped to incorporate the Illinois Indians into his trade network and sought to incorporate the bison hunting tribes like the Otoe of today's Iowa and Missouri.

By mid-winter La Salle had heard nothing about his missing ship. The success of the expedition very much depended on that vessel and all that it carried. Furthermore, at Crèvecoeur his carpenters had run out of rigging, tackle, iron, canvas, and other materials needed to complete the bark.[33] Without these items La Salle could go no further. This serious delay took on greater significance because nearly two years of his five-year license had already elapsed, and he had accomplished very little. Growing ever restless, having heard nothing of his missing bark or the needed supplies it carried, La Salle, in late February, prepared to retrace his steps to his Miami post to learn the status of his *Griffon*. From there he would continue his journey east, first to Niagara, and then to Fort Frontenac where he planned to recruit men and procure supplies.

---

[33] Ibid., 133.

Before leaving Crèvecoeur, La Salle dispatched a party of French up the Mississippi and into Sioux territory. Since it was customary at the time for the French to pair missionaries with secular adventurers during exploratory missions, La Salle determined that one of the three missionaries attached to his expedition, Louis Hennepin, should undertake the voyage with Accault. The explorer also selected Antoine Aguel to accompany the priest and the trader. Of the three clergymen in La Salle's company, Hennepin was best suited for this endeavor: fifty-three years old, adventurous, and anxious to work among the Illinois, he did not, however, know the Miami-Illinois language. The younger and more energetic Father Membré, according to Hennepin, could speak the Illinois tongue, which, if true, would be a valuable skill that the missionaries needed in order to communicate with the Illinois tribesmen near Crèvecoeur. Sixty-year-old Father de Ribourde, the group's spiritual leader, was the least mobile of the three, and thus best suited to remain at Crèvecoeur to perform Mass and meet the spiritual needs of the French.[34]

Hennepin was reluctant to undertake the Mississippi mission. He wrote that he suffered from a "defluxion" in his gums, and he hoped to return to Canada to seek treatment. When his condition improved, he planned to return to Illinois. La Salle, nonetheless, insisted that Hennepin make the journey to Sioux territory. According to Hennepin, La Salle threatened to notify the priest's superiors, telling them that the missionary had "obstructed the good Success of our Mission." He also warned Hennepin, that if he refused the journey, the elderly de Ribourde would be selected to go in his stead. Hennepin found himself caught between two disagreeable alternatives—he could travel to the Sioux country and hope that his condition did not worsen, or he could seek medical treatment in Canada, and by doing so, send his friend, mentor, and master Ribourde on an expedition that he was ill-suited to undertake. Hennepin acquiesced and agreed to accompany Accault. The explorer warmly embraced the priest, and the matter was settled. La Salle gave Hennepin a calumet for safe passage along his route, a few articles for personal use, and several items to give to the Indians as gifts. About this episode Hennepin later wrote, "neither the fair Words, or threats of M. la Salle, would have been able to engage me to venture my Life so rashly, had I not felt within my self a secret but strong Assurance, if I may use that Word, that God would help and prosper my Undertaking."[35]

While Hennepin sought Indians to convert to Catholicism, Accault had been charged with reestablishing relations with the trans-Mississippi tribes. La Salle had given Accault a considerable stock of trading goods valued at between 1,000 to 1,200 *livres*; these would serve as obligatory gifts for the Indians, ensuring that the tribesmen remain in the explorer's trade enterprise. It is also possible that La Salle sent Accault to the Sioux to safeguard his trading relationship from rival Daniel Greysolon Sieur Du Lhut (Duluth), a man who the explorer would later refer to as

---

34 Hennepin in Thwaites, *New Discovery*, 177-178.
35 Ibid., 182.

being "well known as the chief of the Coureurs de bois."[36] Both religious and commercial interests would travel in one canoe, Hennepin with Catholicism and Accault with good will and trade. Just before leaving, La Salle ordered a carpenter to construct a parapet, several oak planks fashioned together to form a shield strong enough to stop arrows on the French canoe's gunwales. With the work completed, the three adventurers set out from Fort de Crèvecoeur on February 29 and paddled down the Illinois.[37]

After encountering two groups of Illinois Indians along the lower stretches of the river, the French arrived at the confluence of the Illinois and Mississippi. There they remained for five days, waiting for ice floes to pass before ascending the Great River. Before the French could reach the Otoe village, they were captured by a Sioux war party on the Mississippi, and were then escorted north, eventually arriving at a Sioux village presumed to be in today's Minnesota. The French were released later that September, most likely due to the commanding demeanor and capable negotiating skills of Du Lhut, who, coincidentally, happened to have been in the Upper Country at the time.[38]

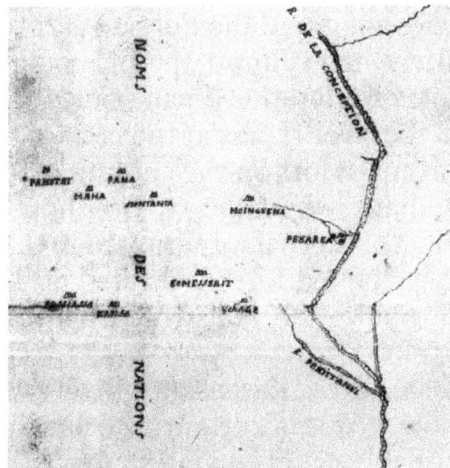

Figure 9: Marquette's 1673 map depicts Otoe and Peoria villages located at or near today's Des Moines River. Marquette, Jacques. [Carte du Mississipi]. 1673-74. Archives de la Société de Jésus Canada Français, Montreal. Recueil 196.

---

[36] Weddle, Morkovsky, and Galloway, *Minet Relation*, 34. Duluth was in the West when La Salle was in the Illinois Country in 1680, having left Montreal in the company of seven men on September 1, 1678. See Duluth in Kellogg, *Early Narratives*, 330, "Remonstrance of Sieur de la Salle against M. de la Barre's Seizure of Fort Frontenac," O'Callaghan, *DCHNY*, IX: 215, and Reuben Gold Thwaites (ed.), *The French Regime in Wisconsin, I—1634-1727*, Collections of the State Historical Society of Wisconsin, vol. XVI (Madison: State Historical Society of Wisconsin, 1902), 110-111. Hereafter cited as Thwaites, *WHC* I.

[37] It is possible that Accault may have paddled down the Illinois in 1678 as he had, besides trading with the Siouan speaking tribes, also traded with the Illinois during the previous year. See Anderson, *Relation of La Salle*, 41.

[38] Their lives were spared when the Sioux saw the calumet that Hennepin carried. Hennepin in Thwaites, *New Discovery*, I: 227-230.

At Crèvecoeur, La Salle was settling his affairs before striking out on his late winter trek to Fort Frontenac. He gathered together his men and implored them to obey Tonti, whom he was leaving in command, to be courageous, and to pay no attention to the false reports and the gossip of the Indians. He told them that he would return soon and would bring with him fresh men, ammunition, and the items necessary to finish the bark.[39] La Salle also directed Tonti to keep the men busy and to mind the store of arms and ammunition. After entrusting Tonti with his personal papers, the explorer left for his seigniory accompanied by Jacques d'Autray, La Violette, Collin, and an Indian hunter.[40] Nothing more could be accomplished at Crèvecoeur as La Salle's men were busy: Hennepin was searching for converts, Accault was renewing old trade contacts, Ribourde was serving the French, and Tonti was in command. To further advance his enterprise, La Salle had to determine the disposition of the *Griffon*.

Snow and rain made La Salle's journey up the Illinois River slow and difficult. His party reached Starved Rock where the explorer likely evaluated the strategic advantages of the bluff. Passing the Rock for the second time, and on this occasion on foot instead of paddling past it, La Salle recognized that the Rock was the most defensible site between Crèvecoeur and the Forks. With steep sides in concert with a towering, small, and relatively flat summit, the site could be defended by a handful of Frenchmen, an important consideration during times of Indian unrest. Additional safety advantages included the river rapids at the base of the bluff, a natural barrier to attackers. Equally important, a fort on the summit would be close to Kaskaskia, home to the thousands of Indians, whom the explorer hoped to both incorporate into his trade network and to enlist as allies if war erupted in the region. It is also possible that La Salle recognized that Starved Rock is located at the lower end of the last of the Illinois River rapids, a realization that would figure into the explorer's plans three years later.

Upon reaching the deserted Kaskaskia village, La Salle's party observed human footprints in the snow. While uncertain as to who had left the tracks, La Salle concluded that they had probably not been made by a war party since the tracks were too few. La Salle assumed that the footprints had been made by a local Illinois hunting party. To avoid an accidental encounter, which could prove to be deadly, La Salle made the decision to announce his party's presence by building a smoldering fire fueled by frosty reeds. The next day, La Salle's efforts were rewarded; the French were approached by three Indians, one of whom was Chassagoac, "the principal chief of the Illinois."[41]

After instructing his men to continue upstream and to wait for him at the Marseilles rapids, La Salle turned his attention to Chassagoac. The explorer began

---

[39] Ibid., 178-179.

[40] The fifteen men included François Boisrondel, three shipwrights, one blacksmith, two joiners, two sawyers, four soldiers, and two Recollet missionaries, Gabriel de Ribourde and Zenobe Membré. La Salle and his group left de Crèvecoeur on March 1, 1680, Anderson, *Relation of La Salle*, 147, 183 and Margry, *Découvertes*, II: 122.

[41] Chassagoac was the "principle chief" of the Illinois village at Lake Peoria. He was not at Lake Peoria when La Salle's party arrived. Anderson, *Relation of La Salle*, 101.

his meeting with the chief by presenting him with gifts, a red blanket, a kettle, and some knives and hatchets, as both an act of friendship and as inducements for the chief's cooperation. Cognizant of the desperate need of food for the men at Fort de Crèvecoeur, La Salle "begged" Chassagoac to bring food to them, offering to pay for provisions when La Salle returned to the Illinois.

La Salle understood that if his enterprise in Illinois were to succeed, it was imperative that he win the confidence and support of Chassagoac. To that end, La Salle told the chief his plans to "put the Illinois upon good terms with the Iroquois, and promising to return soon with a large supply of arms and goods and a greater number of Frenchmen for the purpose of establishing a colony among the Illinois as soon as he should have discovered the mouth of the Great River."[42] From Chassagoac's perspective, La Salle's plans were aligned with those of his people, who very much desired peace. Chassagoac and his people understood that they had little chance of defeating the powerful Iroquois in war. If the Frenchman could convince the Iroquois to accept peace with the Illinois, Chassagoac reasoned, perhaps his people could enjoy a life of safety, security, and stability. This and the prospect of access to trade goods offered significant advantages to his people. Satisfied with the bargain, Chassagoac told La Salle that he would do "everything in his power" to help him. With this understanding, La Salle continued his trek east.

Figure 10: Starved Rock and the frozen Illinois River. Photo by the author.

[42] Anderson, *Relation of La Salle*, 153.

At this point in the narrative we must ask, how much Miami-Illinois language did La Salle know in order to speak to the village chiefs at Lake Peoria, and to have a long and detailed conversation with Chassagoac? As noted previously, La Salle had an exceptional aptitude for languages. But from whom would he have learned Miami-Illinois? Did La Salle stretch the truth when he claimed that he personally spoke to the Illinois chiefs and headmen at Lake Peoria, and had a personal conversation with Chassagoac? Or, are we to take at face value what La Salle's *relation* and other correspondences say about his conversations with the Illinois? An important point to consider is that La Salle had, in 1669, bragged about his ability to speak Iroquoian when, in fact, he did not know the language at all, and this was at a time when he had many contacts with Iroquois speakers.[43]

There is virtually nothing in the known historical record to indicate that La Salle had ever learned Miami-Illinois or that he had ever been exposed to the Miami-Illinois language long enough to have learned it prior to 1680. None of La Salle's travels prior to his arrival at the mouth of the St. Joseph River in late 1679 and his appearance in the Illinois Country a month or so later, would have taken him into lands where Miami-Illinois was spoken. La Salle lived and traveled in country where native languages such as Iroquois, Algonquin-Ojibwe, and Montagnais were spoken, not Miami-Illinois. To this point La Salle mused, while waiting for Tonti to arrive at the St. Joseph fort in November 1679, that he might "win them over [the Illinois] by gifts and good treatment, acquire some smattering of the Illinois language, and by these means the more easily form an alliance with the rest of the nation."[44] Even if La Salle had had access to a Jesuit word list or dictionary, which did not exist until years after the explorer's death, La Salle would not likely have had the components to learn the Miami-Illinois language. According to linguist Michael McCafferty, who has studied the Miami-Illinois language for over forty years, Miami-Illinois is too complex, too difficult for an adult Frenchman to learn without formal instruction in the language. Unfortunately for La Salle, the only French speakers who could have taught the explorer Miami-Illinois were the Jesuits, and La Salle, as we have seen, was an adversary. Further, even though Jesuits Allouez and Marquette could speak the language, having learned Miami-Illinois through immersion, having lived among native Miami-Illinois speakers at mission sites, the formal "mapping out" of the language did not even occur until the 1690s.[45] To communicate with native people, Jesuit missionaries to Canada received formal training as soon as they arrived in the colony in the languages of the tribesmen to whom they would teach, baptize, and minister to.[46] Some Jesuits, including Fathers Gravier and Pinet, later, after the time

[43] René de Bréhant de Galinée in Kellogg, *Early Narratives*, 171.

[44] Anderson, *Relation of La Salle*, 69.

[45] The Miami-Illinois language was later "mapped out" by Jesuit Jacques Gravier who first arrived in the Illinois Country in 1689. Michael McCafferty, linguist, personal communication November 6, 2018.

[46] Marquette spent a year at Trois-Rivières learning native languages under Father Gabriel Druillettes. J. Monet, "Jacques Marquette," *Dictionary of Canadian Biography*, vol. 1 (University of Toronto/ Université Laval, 2003), accessed November 4, 2018 at http://www.biographi.ca/en/bio/marquette_jacques_1E.html).

of La Salle, created whole dictionaries to be used as teaching aides to assist other Jesuit missionaries to show them *how* the Miami-Illinois language actually worked. This was not the case with La Salle as the explorer did not have access to Miami-Illinois dictionaries containing the linguistic road map and mechanisms that are necessary for a student of the language to comprehend or speak Miami-Illinois, nor did he receive any formal training from Jesuit instructors in the Miami-Illinois language.

It appears that at least one, possibly two Frenchmen in La Salle's expedition may have known some Miami-Illinois, or at least knew a few words. According to La Salle, Accault had a "slight acquaintance" with the language, meaning that he knew very little Miami-Illinois and was not conversant in it.[47] Accault may have learned the little Miami-Illinois he did know by direct contact while trading with the Peoria Indians who lived in two villages downstream from the Otoe on the Des Moines River. Accault probably relied heavily on gestures and sign language more than speaking directly to the Peoria, to conduct trade. It seems highly unlikely that Accault's familiarity with or ability to speak Miami-Illinois was sufficient to convey complex notions to the assembled Illinois at the council at Lake Peoria, such as telling the chiefs that "the greater the obstacles" La Salle would overcome "the greater the glory he would gain" for the King of France, or responding to the many claims that Moonswa made to the Illinois against La Salle. Furthermore, Accault was not with La Salle during the explorer's alleged lengthy conversation with Chassagoac.

Another person who could allegedly speak Miami-Illinois, according to Hennepin, was Recollect Father Membré. Like La Salle, how and where Membré could have learned Miami-Illinois is a mystery. Membré arrived in Canada in 1675. It appears that upon landing in the colony, Membré worked as a priest at Beaupré and Trois-Rivières.[48] According to Frédéric Gingras, writing in the *Dictionary of Canadian Biography*, Membré "was chosen to be one of the chaplains on La Salle's first expedition."[49] In other words, Membré was a chaplain, a minister to the French of La Salle's expedition, not a trained missionary who was sent to the Miami and Illinois peoples. There is no evidence available that substantiates Hennepin's claim that Membré could speak Miami-Illinois, or that he had any training in the language whatsoever. Given the lack of evidence and the unlikely timeframe of Membré's sojourn as a parish priest in the Quebec-Trois-Rivières area before joining La Salle, it is doubtful that he knew any Miami-Illinois.

So how did La Salle communicate with the Peoria chiefs and with Chassagoac? Did La Salle have an Indian interpreter with him who knew Miami-Illinois and who could speak to the Illinois on the explorer's behalf? La Salle did have an Indian hunter in his entourage and that Indian accompanied La Salle on his

---

[47] Anderson, *Relation of La Salle*, 117.

[48] Robert S. Weddle, "Zenobe Membré," *Handbook of Texas Online*, accessed November 6, 2018, http://www.tshaonline.org/handbook/online/articles/fme70.

[49] Frédéric Gingras, "Zenobe Membré," in *Dictionary of Canadian Biography*, accessed November 6, 2018, http://www.biographi.ca/en/bio/membre_zenobe_1E.html.

winter trek east after leaving Crèvecoeur. But then, the Indian hunter would have also had to have known French in order to communicate with La Salle. We will see in an upcoming chapter that La Salle employed other Indians, Nanangoucy and Ouiouilamet, for example, who spoke to New England tribesmen on La Salle's behalf. Ouiouilamet, according to La Salle had "acquired a wide knowledge of the languages of the neighboring nations."[50]

Both Allouez and Marquette met, spoke with, and ministered to Illinois Indians at *Pointe du Saint Esprit* mission at today's Chequamegon Bay.[51] The Illinois traveled to the villages there to trade with the Ottawa tribes, many of them Ottawa-Ojibwe speakers. About the Illinois at Chequamegon Bay area, Marquette wrote, "The Ilinois are warriors and take a great many Slaves, whom they trade with the Outaouaks for Muskets, Powder, Kettles, Hatchets and Knives."[52] Clearly, some Illinois had business contacts with Ottawa-Ojibwe-speaking tribesmen.

To facilitate trade, the Europeans and the indigenous groups would have sought some middle ground. "For centuries traders all over the world have traded in languages they did not know and had to learn while trading," writes Huamei Han. However, "we have little knowledge of how they managed to do so."[53] It is certain that some Illinois Indians, who traded with the Ottawa tribes at *Pointe du Saint Esprit*, learned enough Ottawa-Ojibwe to do business with them. But did Nicanapé or the Peoria chiefs know any of the language? Did Chassagoac? Did La Salle's Indian hunter know any Ottawa-Ojibwe? Or, did any of La Salle's men, most of whom were skilled tradesmen from France? If a few of the chiefs at Lake Peoria, or Chassagoac knew at least a little Ottawa-Ojibwe, and if one or two of La Salle's men or his Indian hunter knew a few Ottawa-Ojibwe words, and they supplemented their limited ability to speak with sign language and gestures to make their points known to each other, would it have been possible for all parties to have communicated to some small extent?

La Salle did not know Miami-Illinois but had, by claiming that he had spoken to the Illinois in his correspondences, inadvertently embellished his own linguistic abilities. It is probable that La Salle and the Illinois he encountered made prolific use of gestures, sign language, and drew pictures in the soil to communicate with each other. However, considering the evidence presented, La Salle could not have spoken to the Illinois the way it is portrayed in the written record.

Sometime during the journey, or "on his road," as Tonti had written, La Salle encountered two men whom he had previously dispatched to locate his missing bark. The men told La Salle that his *Griffon* had never arrived at the St. Joseph River post and having traveled around Lake Michigan in search of it, they had neither seen the

---

[50] Anderson, *Relation of La Salle*, 251.

[51] Marquette reported that the Outaouaks gave him "a Young man who had lately come from the Illinois, and he furnished me the rudiments of the language, during the leisure allowed me by the Savages of la Pointe in the course of the Winter." Marquette in Thwaites, *Jesuit Relations*, LIV: 185.

[52] Ibid., LIV: 189.

[53] Huamei Han, "Trade migration and language," in *The Routledge Handbook of Migration and Language*, ed. Suresh Canagarajah (NY: Routledge, 2017), 273.

ship nor learned of its whereabouts.[54] The vessel was missing and the men had been unable to discover why. This devastating news could place La Salle's entire expedition in jeopardy. It was now even more imperative that he reach his seigniory at Fort Frontenac. La Salle directed the two men to join the others at Crèvecoeur and to give Tonti instructions to return to Kaskaskia "to visit a high rock, and to build a strong fort upon it."[55] This dispatch is the first *known* written reference to today's Starved Rock. La Salle's decision to move his headquarters from the Crèvecoeur site to Starved Rock was, in addition to its commercial and geographical advantages, was also influenced by the looming threat of an Iroquois invasion of the country.

Arriving at Fort de Crèvecoeur, the two men relayed La Salle's orders to Tonti. Dutifully following instructions, Tonti left for Starved Rock. During his absence, however, most of the men in his command deserted. Adding to their crime, the deserters stole most of the guns, ammunition, tools, and remaining supplies, leaving only those items too large or too heavy to carry with them. The men even tore down the fort's palisades.[56] The few loyal French who remained, including Tonti, who had returned from reconnoitering Starved Rock, François de Garconnes de Boisrondel, L'Esperance, Etienne Renault, and the missionaries Ribourde and Membré had been left hopelessly stranded in Illinois, without shelter or supplies, and having only enough ammunition to fire "three rounds apiece."[57] Of the 33 crew members who had been with the expedition in January, six remained. None was a skilled woodsman familiar with the ways of wilderness. Had they been, it is still unlikely that they could survive without tools, guns, and supplies. The group's only chance of survival was to seek refuge with the Illinois, who had returned to Kaskaskia. If accepted, Tonti and the others would live at the mercy of the Indians.

It was in April when the French arrived at the Illinois village.[58] Although Tonti had obtained the Indians' consent' to provide for his group, a number of tribesmen remained very suspicious of the French guests. Reflecting on this period, Tonti later wrote that the "desertion of our men, and the journey of M. de la Salle to Fort Frontenac, made the savages suspect that we intended to betray them."[59] Like La Salle with Chassagoac, Tonti understood that his survival, and that of his men, was dependent on the ability of the French to gain the trust of their hosts.

No one knows for certain what Tonti and the French did at Kaskaskia during the summer of 1680. The two missionaries probably baptized attempted to teach and baptize the Indians while also caring for the sick and the dying. Tonti and the others

---

[54] Tonti, in Kellogg, *Early Narratives*, 290. It appears again that Tonti's *Memoir* deviates from La Salle's *Relation*. Tonti wrote that the two men La Salle encountered "on his road" had been sent by the explorer to search for the explorer's missing bark during the previous autumn. La Salle's *Relation*, on the other hand infers that La Salle met these two men at his post on the St. Joseph River, Anderson, *Relation of La Salle*, 157.

[55] Memoir of the Sieur de La Tonty," *Historical Collections of Louisiana*, I: 55 and Anderson, *Relation of Tonty*, 33.

[56] Anderson, *Relation of La Salle*, 169, 199.

[57] Ibid., 188.

[58] Ibid., 233.

[59] Memoir of the Sieur de La Tonty," *Historical Collections of Louisiana*, I: 55.

may have accompanied the Illinois during their summer buffalo hunt, spent time learning their language, and possibly taught Illinois war chiefs a few European military tactics.[60] By September the maize was ready for harvest and subsequent burial in underground storage pits for safekeeping. Clans and family groups were now leaving Kaskaskia and migrating to their winter hunting camps downstream, so many in fact, that by mid-month, only about 2,000 Illinois remained at the village. At about this same time several "Ottawa braves" including a "Kiskakon" and a "Ouinipeg" arrived at Kaskaskia and informed Tonti that La Salle was dead, even providing "proofs pertinent enough" to make him believe that it was true."[61] Although Tonti did not know it at the time, a Huron Indian named Scortas had also told La Salle that Tonti was dead, having been burned alive by the Illinois. La Salle would later learn that his adversary Allouez was again attempting to thwart the explorer's enterprise by spreading lies and attempting to turn the Indians against him.[62] As La Salle's chief deputy, Tonti had to determine if La Salle was dead or alive. Despite the objections of their Illinois hosts who wanted to keep a watchful eye on the French, Tonti loaded a few supplies into a canoe and paddled up the shallow and rocky Illinois River, en route to Michilimackinac. Because the warm Illinois summer had reduced the river to a mere trickle, it was virtually impossible, even by canoe to travel far from the village. Tonti was forced to return to Kaskaskia. Until rainfall raised the level of the river, Tonti would remain there.

Sufficient rain fell a few days later. While Tonti again prepared for the trek to Michilimackinac, a Shawnee Indian who had been visiting Kaskaskia, who was also waiting for rain as his route home took him down the shallow Illinois and up the shallower Vermilion River, took advantage of conditions and left the village that night. Several miles up the Vermilion, he stumbled upon a surprising and dreadful sight—an encampment of about 600 warriors, mostly Iroquois, and an unknown number of Miami. Believing that the Iroquois were preparing to attack Kaskaskia, the Shawnee slipped away into the darkness, unnoticed by the rivals and hurried back to the village to warn his Illinois friends, arriving there early the next morning.

The news of the Iroquois war party seemed to confirm Illinois suspicions regarding Tonti and the French, falsehoods that Allouez had attempted to implant in Illinois minds through his messenger Moonswa earlier that year. Compounding their suspicions was that Tonti was leaving Kaskaskia. One angry Illinois chief approached Tonti and scornfully accused him saying, "We now see plainly that you

---

[60] Evidence for Tonti's teaching of European military tactics to the Illinois is the approach that the Illinois made to the Iroquois camp and battle formations used by the Illinois during the fight. Tonti's portrayal of the battle clearly shows that the Illinois were using European tactics and not Native American ones.

[61] Anderson, *Relation of Tonty,* 27 and Margry, *Découvertes,* II: 297.

[62] Margry, *Découvertes,* II: 297-298.

Figure 11: The shallow and rocky Vermilion River in the vicinity of where the Shawnee encountered the Iroquois war party in September 1680. Photo by the author.

are the friend of the Iroquois." "Now," he continued, "we are dead, for the Iroquois are many and you are their friend."[63] But Tonti, angrily replied, "To prove to you that I am not the friend of the Iroquois, I will die tomorrow with you; I will fight him with the young men who are with me."[64]

The Illinois sent scouts to verify the Shawnee's report, who later returned with confirmation that a large war party was nearby. The scouts also reported that "the leader of the Iroquois," who La Salle later learned was a chief named Teganout, "was dressed in an old Jesuit gown [and] was loaded down with their [the Jesuit's] letters for the Father Allouez."[65] Furthermore, they also reported that La Salle himself was in the war party.[66] To prepare for war, the Illinois sent their women, children, and elderly to a site about eighteen miles downstream to hide in the swampy backwaters. Having safeguarded the noncombatants, the Illinois were faced with a difficult strategic decision: should they wait to be attacked and defend their village, or should they attack the unsuspecting Iroquois first? Although they were outnumbered by a stronger and more organized force, the Illinois had the advantage of surprise. The Illinois were also intimately familiar with the terrain, knowing the layout of the land and the trails and impasses that could facilitate their approach or

---

[63] It had been reported that La Salle was in the Iroquois war party. La Salle was likely at Michilimackinac when the incident took place. Anderson, *Relation of La Salle,* 201, 215.

[64] Anderson, *Relation of Tonty,* 35, 37.

[65] Margry, *Découvertes,* II: 297. Translation by Michael McCafferty of Indiana University, February 5, 2016.

[66] Anderson, *Relation of La Salle,* 201.

retreat from the Iroquois position. The decision was made to attack the Iroquois early the next morning. That night, the Illinois prepared for battle by readying their weapons, performing their war dances, and feasting. In case the enemy captured Kaskaskia, the Illinois reportedly "cast into the river everything that could be of use to the Iroquois," including a few tools, some iron, and a few bits of merchandise that Tonti had been able to salvage from Crèvecoeur.[67]

At daybreak, Tonti and his Illinois comrades crossed the Illinois River, climbed up the steep ravines of today's Starved Rock State Park, and slipped through the tall prairie grass toward the Iroquois camp. Tonti reported, "When the two armies were a half-league apart, the Illinois chiefs begged me to carry a necklace to the Iroquois and to try to make peace with them." Agreeing to do so, Tonti and another Illinois walked some distance ahead of their party, holding the necklace high to alert the Iroquois of their peaceful intentions. The Iroquois, however, were not moved by Tonti's overtures and responded with a volley of musketry. With war clubs, knives, and muskets in hand, the Iroquois charged the Illinois. Tonti implored his Illinois companion to fall back and join the others. An instant later, the rushing Iroquois were upon Tonti. One of the attackers, a Mohegan chief, saw that this buckskin clad emissary was not an Indian at all and cried out, "It's a Frenchman."[68] At about the same time, another warrior lunged at Tonti, knocking him to the ground. In the struggle, the Indian tried to plunge his knife into Tonti's chest. But the blade missed its mark, glancing off a rib. Although the wound was bloody and painful, it was not life-threatening. Another warrior picked up Tonti's hat from the ground and placed it on the end of his gun muzzle, holding it high, a signal to the others that Tonti was dead. But even though he was probably dazed and in a lot of pain, Tonti was still very much alive. The Iroquois next dragged him from the field and brought him before their war captains.

Through a Sauk interpreter who could speak French, the Iroquois chiefs asked Tonti why he had come to them with the necklace. Tonti replied that the Illinois "were under the protection of the King of France and the Governor of the country." He also told them that he was "surprised that they [the Iroquois] wished to break with the French, and to postpone peace."[69] Moments later, a warrior rushed in and told the chiefs that the Illinois had driven back part of the Iroquois line and that Frenchmen were leading the attack. The news visibly irritated the captains as they did not expect Frenchmen, with whom they had a tenuous peace, to be fighting alongside the Illinois. Tonti later wrote that he had:

> never been so much at a loss; for, at the moment when this news came, there stood behind me an Iroquois, knife in hand, who from time to time squeezed me by the hair. I then believed that there was to be no quarter for me, and my greatest hope was that they would knock me in the head, for I thought they meant to burn me.[70]

---

[67] Ibid., 197-199.

[68] Anderson, *Relation of Tonty*, 39. Tonti, an Italian who was wearing buckskins, may have been mistaken for an Illinois Indian by the Iroquois.

[69] Tonti, *Early Narratives*, 291. The French and Iroquois had agreed to terms of peace in 1666.

[70] Anderson, *Relation of Tonty*, 41.

But to Tonti's surprise, one of the chiefs told him he had nothing to fear. Hoping to ascertain the strength of his enemies, the Iroquois asked the Frenchman about the size and composition of the Franco-Illinois force. Knowing that the Illinois had no chance against the Iroquois, and that his own fate was uncertain, Tonti opportunistically misinformed his inquisitors, responding that there were 1,200 Illinois and twenty Frenchmen—a force that more than doubled that of the Iroquois.[71] The news confounded the chiefs. Should they risk a fight that might cause their own defeat, or avoid conflict with both the Illinois and the French? Should they burn Tonti, or should they release him? Deliberating first about Tonti, one Seneca chief, a man named Tegantouki, favored burning him while another chief, an Onondaga named Agostot, who knew La Salle, argued for Tonti's release. A bleeding Tonti watched helplessly while his fate was debated. Agonstot finally persuaded the others to let Tonti live. Next, an Iroquois war chief threw the necklace back to Tonti and ordered him to deliver it to the Illinois as an overture of peace. The chief further instructed Tonti to return with maize to feed the hungry Iroquois warriors. Tonti's simple but convincing deception had thwarted what most assuredly would have ended in a complete Iroquois rout of the Illinois.

Having no intention of supplying the Iroquois with maize, Tonti quickly returned to the Illinois war party, where he was joyfully reunited with Fathers Membré and Ribourde. Soon after, he met with the Illinois chiefs, presented the necklace, and warned them not to trust the Iroquois.[72] The Illinois war party and the French then returned to Kaskaskia with the hostile and belligerent Iroquois following behind. Intimidated and frightened by the Iroquois army, the Illinois warriors left the village and reunited with their women and children downstream.

With the Illinois gone, Kaskaskia, the great Illinois village now belonged to the Iroquois. To defend their conquest from counter-attack, the Iroquois built temporary defensive fortifications, likely sticks and small trees as *abatis*. Having not received the maize that they had demanded of Tonti, the still hungry Iroquois triumphantly pillaged the village maize caches.[73] Two days later, the Illinois returned, appearing at the boundaries of the village, where the two sides exchanged hostages to ensure each other's good faith and behavior. In the following days, an Illinois delegation attempted to secure a peace agreement with the Iroquois war captains, but the Iroquois made no pact with them as they were likely waiting to see if Tonti's exaggerated force of 1,200 Illinois warriors and sixty French soldiers would arrive to liberate the village. Their tactic of waiting was rewarded. Sometime during

---

[71] Tonti, *Early Narratives*, 292. But, Tonti's *Relation*, 41, says that Tonti told the Iroquois that there were 1,100 Illinois and fifty Frenchmen.

[72] There is conflicting information in Tonti's two accounts. In one account, Tonti reported that the Illinois never returned to Kaskaskia after the skirmish. The Illinois were so intimidated by the Iroquois that they left to join their women and children immediately after the fight was over. Anderson, *Relation of Tonty*, 43. Tonti's memoir, however, states that the Illinois returned to Kaskaskia, and then left to join the non-combatants. Tonti, *Early Narratives*, 292.

[73] It is possible that the Iroquois waited until September to attack the Illinois, knowing that the maize would be freshly harvested, in abundance, and could be eaten by their warriors.

the talks, a gullible Illinois delegate revealed to the Iroquois that there was no Franco-Illinois army, and that the Illinois were only about 400 strong. This information transformed the talks from a charade of diplomacy, to one of anger and revenge.

The Iroquois war chiefs summoned Tonti to their cabin, an abandoned Illinois lodge, where he was harshly rebuked for his deception. Fortunate to have escaped his earlier capture, Tonti, again stood before the same chiefs, this time, not as an emissary of peace, on behalf of the Illinois, but as a confirmed liar and enemy of the Iroquois, one who had wrested a victory—the utter destruction of the Illinois—from them, not with warriors and weapons, but with words. Perhaps because Tonti represented the French government, his life was again spared. Tonti and his delegation were ordered to leave the village. The frustrated Iroquois further demanded that the Illinois return the next day to finalize a peace agreement—an arrangement that would be very short-lived.

The next morning, the Iroquois met the Illinois delegation a half league from their Kaskaskia fort. The Iroquois gave the Illinois three gifts, symbolic gestures of peace. The two parties allegedly "bound themselves by oath to a strict alliance, that hereafter they should live as brothers."[74] The Illinois naively believed that the Iroquois were sincere, as the Iroquois later allowed the Illinois to mingle freely in their Kaskaskia village. Conversely, Tonti had serious misgivings about the peace agreement. Asked his opinion of the treaty, a disgusted Tonti told the Illinois chiefs that they "had everything to fear, that there was among these barbarians no good faith."[75] Tonti then pointed to the elm bark canoes that the Iroquois were constructing, vessels that the Iroquois could use to pursue the Illinois should the Illinois decide to flee for their lives downstream. Tonti implored the Illinois to escape quickly to "some distant nation" before the canoes were completed. Tonti was certain that the Iroquois would soon break their pledge of peace with the Illinois.

On September 18, the Iroquois captains summoned Tonti and Father Membré to their lodge. After the two Frenchmen had been seated, the chiefs placed six packets of beaver hides before them. The Frenchmen, presented with the first two packets, were directed to "inform M. de Frontenac [governor of Canada] that they, the Iroquois, would not eat his children and that he should not be angry at what they had done." The third packet was given to represent the plaster for Tonti's stab wound. The fourth packet represented oil "to rub on my own and the Recollect father's limbs, on account of the journeys we have taken." The fifth packet signified the brightness of the sun. The sixth was a strict warning that Tonti and his companions leave for the French settlements the following day. After the Iroquois chiefs finished speaking, Tonti asked the Iroquois when they would leave the Illinois Country. Not only was his question left unanswered, but several captains quipped that "they would eat" some of the Illinois before they left.[76] Realizing that the Iroquois were going to attack the Illinois as soon as the French left the following

---

74 Tonti, *Early Narratives*, 293.
75 Ibid.
76 Ibid.

morning, Tonti kicked the packets away and angrily responded, "I will have none of them," since you plan "to eat the children of the Governor." An angry chief seized Tonti's arm and escorted him out, shouting, "Be Gone!" As the Frenchmen returned to their hut, they could hear the Iroquois delegation singing war songs, a dire warning of what was to come. Anticipating that the Iroquois would kill them, the French waited through the night with knives and guns ready, hoping to kill as many Iroquois as possible before they themselves were slain.

Morning came to Kaskaskia, and the French, alive and unharmed, were allowed to leave. Powerless to help the Illinois, Tonti and the others were indeed fortunate to be leaving literally with their own scalps intact. The Frenchmen, uncertain if they would be pursued by the Iroquois, planned to quickly put distance between themselves and Kaskaskia. Having loaded a few possessions and several bundles of his own personal furs into his canoe, Tonti wrote a letter to the governor that provided the Iroquois with proof that the Iroquois had not killed the French. Tonti gave the letter to an Iroquois chief, pushed the canoe away from shore, and began paddling upriver.

The group traveled about five leagues in the leaky and overburdened craft before they pulled ashore to dry their clothes and cargo. Father Ribourde went into the timber to pray, shunning Tonti's advice to stay with the group. It was now six o'clock in the evening and sunset was fast approaching. Concerned for the missionary's safety, Tonti took up Ribourde's trail, following it for a half-league. Tonti knew the missionary's life was in peril when he saw that his trail had become "confused," mingled in the footprints of Indians, many Indians. Worried about his own personal safety, Tonti returned to camp with the awful realization that the missionary had probably been captured and killed. Leaving their clothes and cargo along the river shore as an incentive for the Indians to steal the goods rather than pursue them, Tonti and the others crossed to the south side of the stream and hid in the underbrush, watching for Ribourde, scanning the river bank, hoping that he had somehow escaped his captors and returned to camp; but this was not to be. The French instead saw some Indians, likely the missionary's abductors, rummaging through their merchandise. In the morning the French crossed the river and while praying for a miracle, vainly waited until noon for Ribourde. The French then boarded their canoes and paddled upstream, traveling as Tonti had written, "by short stages," just in case Ribourde, if he had escaped and lost his way in the woods, would appear. The French continued their journey up the Illinois in this fashion for the rest of the day until a gunshot from the timber made them realize that they were being trailed by Ribourde's killers. They learned later that the old priest had died at the hands of Kickapoo warriors who had been surveilling the area. Today, a stone monument at St. Patrick's Catholic Church in Seneca, Illinois recalls the murder as does the name of a nearby stream, Kickapoo Creek.[77]

---

[77] There are two Kickapoo Creeks near today's Seneca, Illinois. One of them is located on the north side of the Illinois River while the other is located on the south.

Figure 12: Father Ribourde monument located at St. Patrick's Catholic Church in Seneca, Illinois.
Photo by the author.

Tonti's party continued their journey, eventually reaching Lake Michigan. Paddling north from the mouth of the Chicago River, their canoe wrecked at a location thought by some to have been on the shores of today's Door County, Wisconsin. After several harrowing weeks, journeying on foot through frozen wilderness, the party encountered several Frenchmen who were living with Potawatomi Indians. Father Membré was escorted to the St. Francis Xavier mission at Des Pères, Wisconsin by some of these Frenchmen, while Tonti and the others wintered with the Potawatomi. In the spring, Tonti, along with several of his French comrades, left the Potawatomi, and traveled to Michilimackinac.

CHAPTER THREE
SETTING THE RECORD STRAIGHT, MICHILIMACKINAC, AND THE IROQUOIS

While the aforementioned events were occurring in the Illinois Country, La Salle had been quite busy in Canada and on the Great Lakes. He arrived at his Miami post on March 24, 1680. Learning nothing about the status of his bark, the explorer and several companions left the next day for Fort Frontenac. Their route took them overland and across Michigan's Lower Peninsula where they endured cold, sickness, and potential threats from Indians. Eleven days into their trek, two of La Salle's men became so ill that they were unable to continue the journey. The explorer knew that he had to find "some river flowing into Lake Erie, and build a canoe" in order to more easily transport the men.[1] What is interesting about this episode is that it demonstrates, again, that La Salle was a keen observer of his surroundings: he knew that he had crossed a geographical divide where the waters flow east and ultimately into Lake Erie, and not west into Lake Michigan.

La Salle and his group arrived at his Niagara post where he was greeted with more bad news. A ship that he had arranged to deliver goods and merchandise from France had sunk in the Gulf of St. Lawrence, taking with it more than 20,000 *livres* of cargo. Making matters worse, twenty men he had sent for from France who were supposed to join his enterprise had returned to Europe, believing false rumors that the explorer was lost somewhere in the western wilderness. Still unaware of Tonti's situation in Illinois, the explorer dispatched d'Autray and several others to the Illinois Country in two canoes loaded with arms, ammunition, and items needed to outfit his unfinished vessel at Crèvecoeur.[2] La Salle next pushed on with three "fresh men" to Fort Frontenac. Arriving there in early May, the explorer dispatched a crew led by La Forêt to reinforce the men at Crèvecoeur.[3] The explorer then left for Montreal where he likely bartered for trade goods and supplies, and possibly for more credit. A week later, La Salle was en route again to Fort Frontenac where he met two men who had been sent by Tonti to inform the explorer that the men at Crèvecoeur had deserted, looted the storehouse, and demolished the fort's palisades. They also told him that Tonti and the few loyal French had taken refuge with the Illinois at Kaskaskia.[4] The news was troubling. La Salle had borrowed heavily to finance his enterprise. He had lost a ship carrying a small fortune of merchandise

---

[1] Anderson, *Relation of La Salle*, 163

[2] La Salle would meet d'Autray at Michilimackinac a few weeks later as d'Autray no doubt learned about Tonti's predicament in Illinois from Messier and Laurent who were heading east to relay the news to the explorer.

[3] La Forêt would not travel to the Illinois Country at this time as he had been "persuaded," likely by deserters at Michilimackinac that Tonti was dead and to travel to Crèvecoeur would have been useless. Anderson, *Relation of La Salle*, 187.

[4] Ibid., 169.

and supplies. He had hired skilled craftsmen, including carpenters, shipwrights, joiners, and sawyers, and he had paid them large advances, some as high as 1,800 *livres*, only to learn that they had deserted or sailed back to France. In short, he was deeply in debt. The only means to reimburse his creditors was to pay them with the fruits of his success. La Salle had no choice but to take what remained of his enterprise and start anew.

While La Salle prepared to set out for the Illinois again, he learned that some deserters from his expedition had been seen on Lake Ontario. The explorer immediately set out with two groups of men to locate and arrest the fugitives. They eventually captured several deserters, who were subsequently incarcerated at Fort Frontenac. They also killed two others who refused to surrender. La Salle also dispatched an officer to find and arrest another group of deserters who were reportedly headed to New York.[5] Finally, on August 10, 1680, La Salle and twenty-five men began the long and arduous trek back to the Illinois Country. While en route, La Salle met one of his hired men, le Barbier, who had the disagreeable duty of informing La Salle that his bark, the *Griffon* had indeed sunk. It was now official; his vessel was gone and so were 12,000 *livres* of bison hides.

By September, La Salle's canoes had reached Michilimackinac where he planned to purchase maize and dried meat from the Indians. But the Indians refused to sell La Salle the commodities; instead, they offered to sell him beaver hides. La Salle likely figured that this was a trap set by either Allouez, or the Montreal merchants who in 1681 had established a trade post at the site.[6] If La Salle could be enticed into purchasing the illegal pelts, as his patent only allowed him to barter for bison hides, either party could cry foul and accuse the explorer of violating his royal license. Also, by convincing the Indians not to sell La Salle food, whomever had set the trap ensured that his voyage to the Illinois Country would be as uncomfortable as possible, something that might induce more of his men to desert. La Salle refused to violate the terms of his patent. Despite his abysmal financial straits and considering that the money he could have made selling these hides would have helped him monetarily, the explorer remained steadfast in obedience to the king's directives. Fortunately, La Salle did eventually convince some tribesmen to sell him thirty sacks of maize.[7]

At Michilimackinac, La Salle also hoped for good news about Tonti and the Frenchmen with him. Located at the intersection of Lakes Huron and Michigan, the French post there was an important stop in the long chain of French posts and mission sites that linked Montreal with the Illinois Country. Any information coming from the distant west would reach the French at the site sometimes months before it arrived in Montreal. Was Tonti still living at Kaskaskia? Had he left the

---

[5] The deserters were likely en route to a British port where they hoped to board a ship, sail to England, and ultimately return to France.

[6] The trade post at Michilimackinac was established to intercept furs that would have been destined to La Salle's Fort Frontenac. W. J. Eccles, *The Canadian Frontier, 1534-1760* (Albuquerque: University of New Mexico Press, 1974), 114.

[7] Anderson, *Relation of La Salle*, 183.

village to travel to Michilimackinac? Had he been killed? La Salle was to learn nothing new about the status of his lieutenant. Questions about Tonti and what remained of his enterprise went unanswered.

La Salle and his party remained at Michilimackinac for three weeks waiting for canoes bearing supplies and tools, and skilled men whose talents were desperately needed by the explorer. This respite afforded him time to ponder his dreadful situation. Although La Salle had little power to prevent his ships from wrecking, his men from deserting, and Indians from attacking, he could expose the plots of his enemy Allouez and to correct the dishonest and misleading claims of Jolliet. It is during this time that the frustrated explorer penned a letter to Canada Governor Frontenac that, in his view, set the record straight about these two men.

La Salle notified the governor that Great Lakes navigation was not nearly as easy as Jolliet had reported. La Salle wrote, "There are in Lake Erie three large peninsulas, of which two jut out more than ten leagues. These are sand bars which one may run afoul of before seeing them unless one takes great precautions." The next challenge was sailing up today's Detroit River, where "A change of wind is necessary to enter the straits between Lake Erie and Lake Huron, where there is more water and a strong current." Lake Huron, La Salle wrote, has "very few or no anchorages," and few harbors to escape storms and strong winds, a situation made worse by "great numbers of islands" on the lake. Likewise, La Salle reported Lake Michigan had many navigational hazards such as islands and sandbars, the lake is "not deep," and it is "subject to terrific winds from which there is no shelter." Surviving the Great Lakes gauntlet, one next arrives at the mouth of the Chicago River, where the waterway, according to La Salle, is "not at all suitable for navigation as there are no winds in the roadstead, nor any passageway for a vessel, nor even for a canoe, at least in a great calm." Further on, La Salle reported, the prairies near the portage were often "flooded by a great volume of water flowing down from the neighboring hills whenever it rains." And because of this seasonal deluge, the explorer declared that not only would Jolliet's canal be very expensive to excavate, it would "immediately fill up with sand and gravel." And even if Jolliet's canal could be built and maintained, La Salle argued that it would be useless because "the Divine River [combined Des Plaines and Illinois Rivers] is innavigable [sic] for forty leagues, the distance to the Great Village of the Illinois [Kaskaskia]. Canoes cannot traverse it during the summer and even then there are long rapids this side of that village."[8] The explorer also informed the governor, that "there is yet another route, the Ohio, which is shorter and better, and is navigable for sailing vessels." And if a bark sailed the Ohio River instead of the Illinois La Salle wrote, it will avoid the difficulty of Jolliet's "harbor at the end of the lake of the Illinois." These passages clearly demonstrate that La Salle was trying hard to discredit Jolliet's report that the

---

[8] Pease and Werner, *French Foundations*, 2-4.

French "could go with facility to Florida in a bark [from the Great Lakes], and by very easy navigation."[9]

About Illinois Country land, Jolliet had told Dablon, "A settler would not there spend ten years in cutting down and burning the trees; on the very day of his arrival, he could put his plow into the ground." La Salle refuted this claim to the governor, writing, "It should not be supposed that these lands of which we speak in the Illinois are lands to which one has only to put the plow, for the greater part are drowned by ever so little rain." Other Illinois lands, La Salle wrote, "are too dry, and the best require considerable labor to clear off the aspens which cover them, as well as to drain the marshes which comprise wide areas." Countering Jolliet's claim that game animals such as bison are plentiful in the Illinois Country, La Salle replied, "The buffalo are becoming scarce here since the Illinois are at war with their neighbors; both kill and hunt them continually."

Jolliet's explanation for why he and Marquette had not completed their journey to the sea, traveling only as far south as the mouth of the Arkansas River, had been that the two men feared capture by the Spanish. To validate this claim, Jolliet directed that Franquelin's *La Frontenacie* depicted the Spanish as "Europeans" living near the Gulf, in today's Mississippi and Louisiana.[10] La Salle insisted that "There are no Europeans at the mouth of the great river Colbert."[11] The explorer also took exception with how far Jolliet and Marquette had actually traveled down the Mississippi. According to La Salle, "The monster a sketch of which the Sieur Jolliet brought back in a grotesque painted by some Indian of the river: no one will avow its origin. It is a day and a half's journey from Crèvecoeur, and if the Sieur Jolliet had descended a little farther he would have seen another more frightful still." This statement by La Salle implies that Jolliet had not traveled nearly as far south as he had claimed as the "monster" to which he was referring was located near today's Alton, Illinois, about 450 miles north of the Arkansas River. La Salle also refuted the *Frontenacie* depiction of the Mosopela Indians, a tribe that La Salle criticized "were completely wiped out before his [Jolliet's] voyage."[12]

La Salle did not hesitate to challenge and correct Jolliet's claims and remarks about the water route between the Lakes and the Gulf, the Illinois Country, and information that Jolliet provided for *La Frontenacie*. Some of La Salle's counterclaims went beyond mere criticism, to overt contradictions as his later actions concerning his enterprise in the Illinois Country were inconsistent with his reproaches of Jolliet.

---

[9] Ibid., 9. However, La Salle did walk back some of his rhetoric writing that "with more frequent voyages the dangers [one Lake Michigan] will be lessened and the ports and harbors better known. Ibid., 2.

[10] The only Europeans who could have been living in the lower Mississippi at this time would have been the Spanish.

[11] Pease and Werner, *French Foundations*, 4.

[12] Ibid., 5.

Figure 13: Franquelin's 1675 map depicting Europeans at the Gulf and the Mosopela (M8hs8peria). Map courtesy of the Library of Congress: https//www.loc.govresourceg3300.ct000655/.

La Salle next exposed Allouez, accusing the Jesuit of instigating the Miami and the Mascouten to join the Iroquois and to "carry on war against the Illinois."[13] The explorer reported that Allouez' messenger, Moonswa, had attempted to turn the Illinois against La Salle by convincing the tribe that La Salle was planning to destroy them, when in reality, it had been Allouez who was advancing the destruction of the Illinois in order to prevent them from becoming trade partners with the explorer. Even though the explorer was able to convince the Illinois chiefs that Moonswa's accusations were baseless and were intended to sully his name, the explorer still claimed the moral high ground, reporting that he had prevented the Illinois from pursuing and killing Moonswa and his Miami group after they had left the Illinois camp and were returning to their village.

Not only did the explorer accuse the Jesuit of inciting the Miami to join the Iroquois and attack the Illinois, La Salle also informed the governor that as a missionary, Allouez' impact among the Illinois was negligible at best. The explorer reported that he had seen only three Christian Indians, and these were children, not adults. In fact, La Salle predicted that these children would eventually leave the faith and grow up to be like their polygamist father. He wrote that Allouez had turned his back on his Illinois flock, leaving only his walking staff with them, insinuating that the "extraordinary [supernatural] powers" of the relic qualified as a sufficient substitute for his presence.[14] La Salle sarcastically equated Allouez's staff to the one carried by Moses, a talisman that he was said to have carried when he parted the Red Sea, extracted water from a rock, and defeated the Amalekites at Rephidim.

---

[13] Pease and Werner, *French Foundations,* 11. The Wea are a Miami subtribe.
[14] Ibid., Translation by Michael McCafferty.

If La Salle's accusations against Allouez are credible, it is inexplicable that the Jesuit incited the Miami to join the Iroquois against the Illinois. Why would the Jesuit seek to destroy the very tribe to which he had ministered and had worked so hard to earn their trust? Could it be that Allouez so despised La Salle and what he represented that he was willing to sacrifice his own converts to keep the explorer out of his missionary domain? Or, is it possible that the Jesuit knew that even if the Iroquois attacked the Illinois, he could use the incident to his advantage by convincing the tribe that they needed to seek the protection and favor of his Christian god.[15] Fortunately for the Illinois, it appears that only a small number of Miami were convinced to join the Iroquois and take up arms against them.

In addition to La Salle's suspected maneuvering by Allouez, it appears that La Salle also suspected that other Jesuits had a hand in sabotaging his bark, the *Griffon*.[16] According to one informant, La Salle planned to avenge the crime by dispatching two men to Michilimackinac to trade with the local tribes. After accumulating a supply of hides, the two men would leave them in the custody of the Jesuits. After these priests and their *donnés* had transported the peltry to Montreal, La Salle would appear, catch the Jesuits with the hides, and report the clerics to authorities. The proposed trap to catch the Jesuits was never set.[17]

La Salle's polemic to Frontenac was written when nearly every aspect of his enterprise was coming apart. He took aim at Jolliet, whose report to Dablon and *Frontenacie* map led La Salle to believe that the Illinois River was a navigable waterway. La Salle wanted to crush whatever credibility and political clout his perceived rival might have. He also wanted secular authorities in Canada to know that Allouez and other Jesuits were not only interfering in French business affairs, they were actively engaged in inciting tribal warfare, something that not only affected La Salle, it destabilized intertribal relations that could potentially threaten Canada's fur trade.

By October 4, 1680, La Salle could no longer wait for the supplies, tools and men to arrive at Michilimackinac. Tonti needed help and the explorer was the only Frenchman who could render him aid. Winter would soon be upon the Lakes, making travel difficult, miserable, and dangerous. With twelve men, La Salle left Michilimackinac for the Illinois Country.

On December 1, La Salle and his group arrived at Kaskaskia. There they beheld the complete destruction of the Illinois village by the victorious Iroquois. In the village burial grounds, graves had been ravaged. Packs of wolves gathered to feed on the decaying bodies that had been "dragged from graves and scattered about the plain." Wolves gathered to feed on the decaying bodies that had been dragged from graves and scattered about the plain.[18] The Iroquois had burned and looted the

---

[15] A lesson learned by the Jesuits in upper Lakes when the Ottawa tribes fled *Pointe du Saint Esprit* to escape the Sioux. See Thwaites, *Jesuit Relations*, LVII: 207.

[16] For an example of one of La Salle's accusations against other Jesuits, see Margry, *Découvertes*, II: 295-296.

[17] Weddle, Morkovsky, and Galloway, *Minet Relation*, 34.

[18] Anderson, Relation of La Salle, 223.

entire village. La Salle was deeply troubled by what he saw. Not only did Kaskaskia lie in ruins, the Illinois had been run out of the Illinois Valley by the Iroquois conquerors, and there was no trace of Tonti or the French.

Although written documents are unclear about what La Salle and his men did next, the best evidence seems to indicate that they boarded their canoes and cautiously paddled down river, on guard in the event that the Iroquois warriors still patrolled the area. After traveling about five miles, La Salle's men disembarked on the south shore of the river at a stream that enters the Illinois. Finding a "rock-hollow" that was reportedly "very hard of access," in a crevice, according to the best French translation, La Salle's men stashed their belongings to disencumber themselves of the extra weight.[19] The explorer, d'Autray, and the rest of the French group then set up camp and readied themselves to begin their search for Tonti and the others the next morning. La Salle also directed three of his men to "retire to a neighboring island," a site reportedly located between two rapids, where the men were instructed to place themselves on the "eastern point," in order to keep "a sharp lookout" on the hidden merchandise.[20] With the cargo tucked away safely on shore and with sentries guarding the goods, La Salle, d'Autray, Hunaut, You, and an Indian companion paddled down the Illinois the next morning in search of what remained of his lost expedition.

La Salle's party arrived at a site located on the north side of the river where the Illinois had directed their women and children to hide just prior to the skirmish with the Iroquois. Across the stream, the French saw the remains of an Iroquois camp. The explorer and his men searched the Illinois site, looking for any sign of Tonti or the others. Finding none, the party spent the night at the abandoned Iroquois camp. Continuing their trek downriver the next morning, the group arrived at the remains of Fort de Crèvecoeur. The deserters had, as La Salle had been informed, "demolished" the fort. He also saw that the passing Iroquois war party had contributed to the plunder by pulling the nails from the unfinished bark, an act that was meant to send a message to the explorer that the Iroquois not only resented his meddling in Illinois Country affairs, they also resented what the bark represented in terms of disrupting the flow of peltry that they had grown used to obtaining from western tribes. Leaving Crèvecoeur, La Salle's party continued downstream, passing the campsites of the retreating Illinois and on the opposite shore, those of the Iroquois. It appears that as the Illinois retreated downstream, their group became larger and larger as they encountered other Illinois groups who had left Kaskaskia for the winter hunt before Tonti and the remaining Illinois had encountered the Iroquois. But unlike the Iroquois war party that was comprised of 582 physically fit and well-conditioned warriors, the larger Illinois group consisted primarily of women, children, and the elderly.[21]

It seems odd that rather than attack the fleeing Illinois before the Illinois group became too large to strike, the Iroquois war party, instead, chose to follow the

---

[19] Anderson, *Relation of La Salle*, 227, 229.
[20] Ibid.
[21] Ibid., 231.

Illinois group and intimidate them. The question is, why would nearly 600 Iroquois warriors, most of them having traveled over 600 miles to raid Kaskaskia, not have struck the fleeing Illinois group before it became too large to attack? It is possible that while the Illinois used *mihsoori*, large, stable wooden dugout canoes to travel downstream to flee the Iroquois, the Iroquois who pursued them used fragile, leaky, and less stable elm bark canoes, the same ones that Tonti saw them constructing at Kaskaskia. Perhaps having to stop intermittently during their chase to repair leaks and empty water that had seeped into their craft, the Iroquois, or at least some of them, arrived too late in the day to attack their fleeing enemies. Or possibly, the Illinois at Kaskaskia had fled their village before the Iroquois had completed construction of enough canoes to pursue them, which caused the Iroquois to chase the Illinois in a strung out, piecemeal fashion. But for whatever reason, both the Illinois and the Iroquois eventually found themselves in a stalemate of sorts, a situation that neither side likely hoped would erupt into open warfare. Regardless, the Iroquois continued to menacingly stalk and shadow their Illinois adversaries down the river.

When the Illinois Indians finally reached the Mississippi, it appears that the Kaskaskia, Cahokia, and Chinkoa subtribes ascended the river while the Omouhoa, Coiracoenanon, Moingoana, and Chepoussa subtribes descended it.[22] The Peoria crossed the river, returning to a place that was very familiar to them, their old villages near the Des Moines River in northern Missouri, located at today's Illiniwek State Historic Site, where Marquette and Jolliet encountered them in 1673.[23]

While the Illinois groups fled to new camps, the Tamaroa, Tapouaro, and Espeminkia women and children were savagely attacked by the Iroquois army while the men, according to La Salle, had been away hunting. When it was over, about 350 lay dead and mutilated while another 350 were marched to Iroquois territory as slaves.[24] It seems incomprehensible that the men of these subtribes remained east of the Mississippi to hunt while leaving their women and children unprotected, and this after having been pursued by the Iroquois for over 200 miles. La Salle's *Relation*, the principal source of this incident, is a narrative strung together by one of his supporters in France, the Abbé Claude Bernou. Based on letters that the explorer had sent to the priest, the *Relation* states "the Moroas or Tamaroas, the Tapouaros, and the Ispeminkias, more credulous than any of the other Illinois, remained near the mouth of their river, intending to hunt in that neighborhood."[25] Although La Salle, through communication provided to the abbot, blames the credulity of the Illinois men for the massacre, there could be another more plausible explanation.

---

[22] Ibid., 215 and Zitomersky, *French Americans*, 88.
[23] Wayne Temple, *Indian Villages of the Illinois Country*. Illinois State Museum Scientific Papers, vol. II, part 2 (Springfield: Illinois State Museum, 1966), 24 and Larry Grantham, "The Illini Village of the Marquette and Jolliet Voyage of 1673," in *The Missouri Archaeologist* vol. 54 (1996): 1-20.
[24] Anderson, *Relation of La Salle*, 215.
[25] Ibid.

In 1680, about 200 families of Tamaroa (1,000 people) lived in a village along the Mississippi, approximately seven leagues below the mouth of the Illinois.[26] It seems quite possible that these Tamaroa were not part of the larger Illinois group that fled Kaskaskia at all, but instead had been hunting in their home territory, oblivious of the Iroquois attack at Kaskaskia and the subsequent pursuit of the other Illinois sub tribes down the Illinois River, when the Iroquois appeared in their midst. Considering this, it would have been reasonable for the Tamaroa to have left their women and children unprotected while the men were away hunting because they did not know that the Iroquois were in the area. In fact, the Iroquois route back to their Upstate New York villages, up the Ohio River, would have coincidentally taken them past a Tamaroa village. Additionally, it is possible that the "Tapouaro" and the "Ispeminkia," too, may not have been part of the Illinois group that fled before the Iroquois.[27]

Having now achieved two important military objectives, namely striking a blow to their Illinois enemies and driving them from their territory, and thereby depriving La Salle of their support, the Iroquois began their long trek home.

Finding the massacre site, La Salle and his men rummaged through the charred and mutilated corpses, searching for the remains of Tonti and his party. Failing to locate them, the Frenchmen placed a board at the mouth of the Illinois River that advised Tonti, should he pass the site, that he, La Salle, had returned upstream and that he had hidden some goods, knives, hatchets, and other items, should Tonti need them. La Salle and his party then began the journey back north to reunite with his men on the island.

La Salle acknowledged that his enterprise was in even more peril, now that the Illinois had been driven from Kaskaskia and the Illinois Valley. He could do little without these hunters and potential partners and allies. To be successful in his western venture, it was imperative that he convince the Illinois to return to their villages despite all that had occurred. Moreover, half of La Salle's five-year patent had already expired. He would leave the Illinois Country and travel to safer lands where he would reassess his situation in Illinois, recruit men, and determine how to overcome the seemingly overwhelming obstacles that threatened every aspect of his Western enterprise.

Reunited with the men upstream, La Salle and his group spent the next eighteen days camped next to the rock-hollow and crevice where they had hidden their goods and supplies. During this time, some of the explorer's men returned to Kaskaskia to gather maize from fields that had escaped the fiery wrath of the Iroquois. Others busied themselves felling trees, splitting logs, and building sledges to carry their merchandise and canoes over the now frozen Illinois River and out of the Illinois Country. When their work was completed, the French loaded their possessions onto their sledges and began the frigid march upriver. Upon reaching the Forks, La Salle chose to ascend the Des Plaines because he had stumbled upon a campsite on the north side of the river that, he surmised, had been used by Tonti

[26] Ibid., 119, and Hennepin in Thwaites, *New Discovery*, 183.
[27] The 1684 Franquelin map depicts the Tapouaro living in on a river in present-day Iowa.

during his flight from the Illinois Country. After pushing, pulling, and prying the cumbersome sledges up the rocky and semi-frozen Des Plaines, the exhausted French landed on an island where they unloaded their sledges and hid their merchandise in the brush. There, d'Autray and a man known only as the "surgeon," possibly Jean Michel, remained to guard the goods while La Salle and the others continued their journey to the explorer's Miami post.[28] The island where the goods and supplies were stored may possibly be the site known today as Isle à la Cache (literally, Island with the Hiding Place), located at today's Romeoville, Illinois.[29]

---

[28] A *surgeon* named Jean Michel was attached to La Salle's 1682 Gulf expedition. *The Journeys of Rene Robert Cavelier Sieur de La Salle*, 2 vols., ed. Isaac Joslin Cox (New York: Allerton Book Company, 1906), I: 170.

[29] Anderson, *Relation of La Salle*, 243. Isle à la Cache was known by that name as early as 1698 as referenced by the French missionary Jean-François Buisson de St. Cosme. See Kellogg, *Early Narratives*, 349.

CHAPTER FOUR
LA SALLE REGROUPS, 1681-1682

With every passing moment, the likelihood diminished that La Salle could overcome a seemingly endless series of catastrophes, and yet establish his fort at the Gulf. It was imperative that he quickly revitalize his enterprise in the short time that remained of his patent. To do this, La Salle had to accomplish several important objectives. First, he had to convince the Illinois to return to Kaskaskia. Second, he had to mend the intertribal rift between the Illinois and Miami and persuade the two tribes to join forces and live together peacefully. He also had to locate the Gulf via the Mississippi, reconnoiter the route along way, and claim the region for France.

La Salle arrived at his Miami fort in late January. To his disappointment, Tonti was not there, but his close associate La Forêt, and three soldiers, part of the group that was supposed to rendezvous with the explorer in the Illinois Country the previous fall, were. Also at the post were 25 to 30 warriors and their families, displaced Indians from New England who had come to Miami country to hunt. Their contempt for the British combined with having few trade opportunities due to the scarcity of beaver in their country had forced these tribesmen to consider surrendering their sovereignty to the Iroquois in order to survive. Nanangoucy, an Indian in La Salle's employ, convinced them first to meet with the explorer to see what La Salle might offer them. Before he would meet with the northeastern tribes at the Miami post, La Salle determined that he must first return to the Illinois Country to convince the Illinois to return to Kaskaskia. Next, he had to find d'Autray and the surgeon, who were guarding the merchandise on the island, and escort them and their load of goods back to the St. Joseph post. After these objectives had been accomplished, La Salle would meet with New England tribesmen. To ensure that the northeastern Indians already gathered around his post remained at the site while he was away, La Salle instructed another Indian helper, Ouiouilamet, to begin negotiations with them to convince them to remain in Miami country.

While La Salle was making preparations to leave for the Illinois Country, a Shawnee chief from the Ohio Valley and 150 of his warriors appeared at the post to beseech the explorer for French protection from the Iroquois. La Salle communicated to the chief that if the chief would accompany him to the mouth of the Mississippi, the explorer would place him and his people under the suzerainty of the French king. The chief gladly accepted La Salle's offer to travel to the Gulf and promised the explorer that he would rendezvous with him in the fall, at the Miami post.[1]

On the first day of March, 1681, La Salle and fifteen men, one of them La Salle's Indian associate Ouiouilamet, left the St. Joseph post for the Illinois Country. Travel was relatively easy on snowshoes as the late winter snow was reported to have been "solidly frozen." The crust of snow also made chasing game easy for a pack of hunting

---

[1] Anderson, *Relation of La Salle*, 259.

dogs that accompanied La Salle's group, animals that reportedly "were killing for him as many deer and other animals as he [La Salle] wanted."[2] But even though travel conditions in this part of the Illinois Country were optimal and the group had plenty to eat, La Salle's eyes had no protection from the steady glare of the sun's rays reflecting off the snow's icy coating. He was stricken with snow blindness for three days. Instructing most of his group to continue their search to locate the Illinois, the explorer decided to stay behind at a makeshift camp, likely located somewhere in today's northeastern Illinois, until his eyesight returned. While La Salle sat idle, Hunaut, a Frenchman who remained with the explorer, left camp to search for pine needles to treat La Salle's afflicted eyes. While away, he discovered several sets of footprints in the snow. Returning to camp, he told La Salle what he had seen. The explorer knew that it was imperative that he determine who made the impressions; he did not want the French to be mistaken for enemies. Hunaut and Ouiouilamet volunteered to find out where the tracks led and to speak to whomever had made them. La Salle, unable to travel due to his condition, allowed the men leave to search for the people who made the tracks.

For two full days and most of a third the two men followed the trail until they arrived at a Mesquakie hunting camp, eighty cabins in all. Announcing their arrival before the village, the men were greeted by the tribesmen and escorted inside. Sometime after discussing the purpose of their visit, La Salle's men learned that Tonti was alive and living among the Potawatomi in Wisconsin. The Mesquakie also told them that Hennepin, Accault, and Aguel had been captured by the Sioux but were now safe. Leaving the Mesquakie camp, Hunaut and Ouiouilamet returned to the French camp to report to La Salle. Reenergized at the good news, and with his vision restored, the explorer was ready to continue his search for the Illinois.[3]

Likely following the Illinois River downstream, La Salle's party met the group that the explorer had sent in advance. It was mid-March, and as the temperatures began to warm, the ice choking the river began to break apart and drift away. Taking advantage of conditions, La Salle's men made several canoes, likely wooden dugouts, or *pirogues* as the French called them, to travel the river. Continuing their search downstream, the men eventually had a chance encounter with ten Illinois Indians hunting near Kaskaskia, of which at least one of whom may have been a chief.[4] La Salle gave them a few gifts to console them for their recent loss at the hands of the Iroquois. He then, likely through his interpreter, beseeched the Illinois to end their feud with the Miami and to unite with them to better defend themselves against the Iroquois, their mutual enemy. The explorer tried to explain to the Illinois that "so long as they [the Illinois and Miami] remained divided, the Iroquois would despise them and would defeat them separately." La Salle communicated to them that "if they would come to terms they would become

---

[2] Ibid., 259-261. Translation from the French by Michael McCafferty. Tonti and the French with him used dogs to find and kill game while traveling between today's Lake Simcoe and La Salle's Miami post, Weddle, Morkovsky, and Galloway, *Minet Relation*, 41. Hunting dogs were also used by the Miami Indians. See Margry, *Découvertes*, II: 319.

[3] Anderson, *Relation of La Salle*, 263.

[4] The encounter must have occurred near Kaskaskia as the French later obtained "a hundred *minots* of Indian corn," a quantity that could have only come from large agricultural village such as Kaskaskia. Ibid., 265.

invincible and formidable to all their enemies, as he [La Salle] would come to settle among them with other Savages and many Frenchmen."[5] The Illinois thanked La Salle for his concern and took his message back to their village, where they relayed what they had learned from La Salle to their chiefs and elders. The next day, the explorer and his men boarded their canoes and traveled up the Illinois. Reaching the Forks, La Salle retraced his January route up the Des Plaines River where he found d'Autray, the surgeon, and the goods cached on the island. La Salle instructed several of his men to hurry to Wisconsin to find Tonti, and to retrieve from him his papers that were, hopefully, still in his custody. La Salle and the rest of his group then paddled back to the St. Joseph post.

Figure 14: A pirogue or dugout canoe. Likely a discarded replica, it was discovered by Illinois Conservation Police near the Forks of the Des Plaines and Kankakee Rivers in 2005. Photo by the author.

That La Salle felt it was, at this point, more important to find the Illinois and speak with them before he met with the New England and Miami tribes is very telling. It demonstrates that the Illinois were central to the success of his enterprise. Their claimed territory had been within the range of mid-seventeenth-century bison migrations, the tribe were bison hunters, and they lived in villages located along the Illinois and Mississippi Rivers, major waterways that flowed to the Gulf. La Salle understood that the Illinois Indians were the linchpin required to hold together a successful enterprise.

Arriving back at the Miami post, La Salle dispatched a second canoe, one under the direction of La Forêt to complete several important tasks. La Forêt was instructed to find Tonti and instruct him to wait for La Salle at Michilimackinac. La Forêt was

---

[5] For La Salle to have beseeched ten common Illinois men to end their wars with the Miami would have been futile. Ibid., 263.

ordered to travel then to Fort Frontenac to gather goods, ammunition, and fresh men, and to then return to Michilimackinac to await the explorer.

While La Forêt was away, La Salle and the men with him busied themselves clearing timber around his post and planting crops. As they toiled in the woods and fields, several New England tribesmen arrived to inform La Salle that they were patiently waiting at the Miami village for him to speak with their chiefs. La Salle and several Frenchmen soon boarded canoes and paddled to the Miami village to meet these Indians.

That La Salle made no effort to meet with the New England tribes or the Miami after returning to the St. Joseph, and that he had to be reminded to do so, is intriguing. Although it is possible that some of the tribesmen had not yet returned from the winter hunt, and that La Salle was waiting for their arrival before addressing the chiefs, a better explanation would be that the explorer had intended for these tribes to play a supporting role in his enterprise. La Salle likely figured that if he did not mend relations between the Illinois and Miami, the Iroquois would continue their raids and not only weaken the fragile trade alliance he was trying to establish, they could possibly destroy it altogether. The Illinois would need the Miami as partners to help defend their territory from the Iroquois. Further, if La Salle could convince the New England tribes to join him rather than submitting to the Iroquois, he would have effectively deprived the Five Nations of manpower and support and would have successfully diverted those resources to himself.

Not long after La Salle arrived at the Miami village, he saw three Iroquois, probably warriors who were returning to their homelands after having participated in the attack on the Illinois. La Salle knew that they were at the village for one purpose, to incite the Miami against the Illinois and thereby derail his plans. When the Iroquois saw La Salle they welcomed the explorer, greeting him as a friend. However, La Salle was not fooled by their cajoling; he had learned that before he had arrived the Iroquois had been speaking contemptuously about the French. La Salle reportedly, "received them coldly, telling them that they had spoken amiss of a nation they were bound to respect [the Illinois]," indicating that with French and Miami assistance, the Illinois would be more powerful than they. La Salle, who was surrounded by an entourage of French woodsmen and some New England tribesmen, also told the Iroquois that they did not have the courage to say to him what they had been saying about the French to the Miami. Outnumbered and intimidated, the Iroquois later left the village, silently slipping out unnoticed in the night, and leaving their personal belongings behind. The Miami too were impressed by the explorer's bravado. This incident is credited with sparking renewed interest in a Miami relationship with La Salle both in what the explorer could offer the Miami and in his overtures of intertribal peace and unity.[6]

La Salle later summoned together the "Moraigane," "Anhanagane," Mohegan, and the "Minissens" and other New England Indians who were eager to hear the explorer's proposals to them.[7] To these tribes he communicated the advantages of settling in the Illinois and Miami Country. Likely through his interpreters Nanangoucy

---

[6] Ibid., 269.
[7] These tribes included the Moraigane, Anhanagane, Mahigane (likely Mohegan), and the Minissens. Margry, *Découvertes*, II: 148.

and Ouiouilamet, he told them that the land was fertile, and that game and fish were abundant. He promised they could live without fear, far away from their British enemies, under the protection of the French king. However, La Salle informed them that before their move to the new country, he would first have to "discover" the mouth of the Mississippi in order to deliver to them "all sorts of goods very cheaply," along with horses and cattle and other items they had enjoyed in their former homelands. For their part, La Salle insisted that they help him reconcile the Illinois and Miami. He conveyed to the tribesmen that war between the two tribes would disrupt stability. La Salle's propositions were enthusiastically accepted by the Indians. They agreed to work with the explorer to mend the ongoing rift between the Illinois and Miami and in the process, become part of La Salle's new Franco-Indian alliance.

The next day La Salle met with the Miami. With much drama and fanfare, he presented the tribe twelve gifts, each with its own symbolic message. In the twelfth and final gift, La Salle represented the King of France and his will concerning the Miami people: "He who is the master of life and of the whole earth is a very great captain. He is potent and feared throughout the world; he loves peace and desires us to hear his words which are for our preservation and our greatest good."[8] That person, La Salle communicated to them, was "the King of France... whose kindness extends even to your dead." He let them know that they must never go to war without the consent of "Onontio," the governor of Canada, and that they must live peacefully with their Illinois neighbors. After the meeting, the chiefs met in council to discuss the merits of the explorer's proposals.

The following day, the Miami assembled in front of La Salle's lodge where they presented the explorer with five gifts, each of them consisting of ten beaver skins that represented a particular message. The third gift represented their willingness to lay down their arms, break their arrows, and bury their tomahawks deep in the ground in order to establish peace between themselves and the Illinois.[9] This was a major success for La Salle, one that not only helped to coalesce his plans, but it also was an important step to repair the damage to intertribal relations that had been instigated by certain Jesuits. The tribe then symbolically placed themselves under the authority of the king of France; they hoped that the Illinois could be convinced to do likewise.

The other gifts presented to La Salle reveal clues that might explain the strange relationship between the Miami and the Iroquois, two tribes with little in common, who at times fought together, and who now appeared to be on a collision course. According to their spokesman, the Miami had given the Iroquois "more than three thousand beaver skins" to ransom the bones of a deceased Miami chief named Ouabicolcata. It is unclear if the spokesman was speaking literally, that the Iroquois had indeed stolen the bones of their deceased chief, or metaphorically in that the Miami were required to pay tribute to the Iroquois in order to remain in their territory, land that was once the domain of their deceased chief. Either way, in the words of the Miami spokesman, the Iroquois "have stripped us of everything."

---

[8] Anderson, *Relation of La Salle*, 263-281. La Salle in Pease and Werner, *French Foundations*, 11.
[9] Ibid., 289.

For the moment, the Miami agreed to accept La Salle's offers. Their decision injected another sorely needed shot of optimism for the explorer, who still hoped that his western venture might still be successful. The understanding between the Miami and the Illinois and the cooperation of the Shawnee, as well as the northeastern tribes, all auspiciously contributed to the prospects of a stable and profitable enterprise. More assurance came with La Salle's new crew of Frenchmen. Unlike those who he had hired in 1678, these were experienced woodsmen—hardened, resourceful, and accustomed to the harsh realities of the wilderness. Ready to move forward, La Salle could now focus on reaching the Gulf, hoping to set out with his Franco-Native American entourage in autumn 1681.

Leaving the St. Joseph in late May, La Salle traveled to Michilimackinac to rendezvous with La Forêt, who should have been there waiting for him. He was not, having left the post and returned to Fort Frontenac a second time to tend to unofficial business.[10] La Salle was exasperated by La Forêt's untimely and unwarranted absence, but his anger soon abated when he was reunited with Tonti and Father Membré.[11] The men did not have time to celebrate: they had to get to Fort Frontenac to find out what had become of La Forêt. Tonti and Membré left Michilimackinac and traveled with La Salle as far as Teyagon, a village believed to have been on an island in Ontario's Lake Simcoe, where Tonti expected to intercept a boat carrying supplies and merchandise and to get it to the Miami post.[12] La Salle continued east. Arriving at his seigniory, the explorer was handed several letters, directives from Governor Frontenac instructing him to report to Montreal. Dutifully following orders, and despite the fact that this was yet another delay that would cost him even more precious time, La Salle continued to Montreal, a pointless waste of time as the governor never arrived.[13] In the meantime, Tonti had completed his assignment at Lake Simcoe and was canoeing to the St. Joseph with fresh men and a load of materiel. La Salle would, as soon as time and distance allowed, rendezvous with Tonti and the others there.

Eventually La Salle arrived at his St. Joseph post and by late January he and his entourage of Indian men and women and Frenchmen were ready to make the cold winter trek to the Gulf. Leaving the fort, the convoy skirted the south shore of Lake Michigan, intending to take the familiar Chicago-Des Plaines-Illinois River route. La Salle's party stalled at the Chicago Portage because the winter's cold had closed navigation of the waterways of northern Illinois. In order to travel faster when the rivers

---

[10] La Salle instructed La Forêt to meet him on May 1. However, La Salle did not leave the St. Joseph post until May 25. See Ibid., 265 and 297.

[11] There is some confusion in the accounts as Anderson's *Relation of La Salle*, 297, states that La Salle had reunited with Tonti at Fort Frontenac, while Tonti's Memoir in Kellogg, *Early Narratives*, 296, states that they were reunited at Michilimackinac.

[12] Kellogg, *Early Narratives*, 296 and ff. The Lake Simcoe route was used by the French as a shortcut between Lake Erie and Lake Huron that avoided the strong currents in the Detroit River.

[13] According to one of the Minet *Relation* informants, La Salle had borrowed a large sum of money from his brother Jean. La Salle paid his brother back in illegal pelts, hides that were in violation of his royal patent. When the plot became known, spies were sent out to "nab" La Salle if he returned to Montreal. The informant said that at this time, La Salle traveled "secretly" to Montreal to purchase merchandise, not to meet with the governor.

allowed passage, the explorer elected to lighten their load by burying merchandise and supplies that he felt were non-essential for the expedition somewhere near the portage for safekeeping. The French also began building sledges to haul their canoes and other items downriver. Rather than drag or carry their canoes down the frozen streams, the Indians in the party, instead, chose to disassemble theirs and haul them over ice in pieces. Leaving the portage, the Franco-Native American group reached the Des Plaines River and walked that stream to the Illinois, eventually passing the abandoned Kaskaskia village and Starved Rock. At last, they reached open water at Lake Peoria, from where the group continued their trek downriver in canoes until they reached the Mississippi. La Salle's group set up camp at the mouth of the Illinois where they remained for about twelve days waiting for ice floes to pass and the continuous rains to abate.

It was at this Illinois Country location that La Salle's compass, the only one he possessed, had allegedly become broken. This apparent misfortune, whether it is true or not, theoretically meant that he could not ascertain whether his party was traveling due south or due north. He was, however, able to determine his latitude as he had with him a seven-inch-long astrolabe.[14] The broken compass may figure significantly into mistakes found on Jean-Baptiste Franquelin's *1684 Carte de la Louisiane*, a map that includes the lands and waterways traversed by La Salle during the years 1679 through 1682.

The group continued their voyage. Twelve leagues below the mouth of the Illinois, they stopped at an abandoned Tamaroa village located on the east shore of the river. Knowing that he would pass their village on his return north, and to let them know that he and his entourage were friendly and not Iroquois, La Salle left them a quantity of glass beads and several hatchets.

Five days after leaving the confluence of the Mississippi and Illinois, the explorer's group passed the mouth of the Ohio River. With the exception of the expedition's blacksmith, Pierre Prudhomme, who became lost in the timber while hunting (presumably near today's Memphis), and a close encounter with about 100 Natchez warriors somewhere along the lower Mississippi, the remainder of the journey to the Gulf was relatively uneventful.

La Salle's party eventually reached a point on the Mississippi where the river separates into three channels. La Salle instructed Tonti and d'Autray to each lead a group down one of the channels while he would lead a third. The three groups arrived at the Gulf on April 6, 1682. At a ceremony held three days later, La Salle claimed the entire Mississippi Valley, effectively, everything and everyone between the western slopes of the Appalachians to the eastern slopes of the Rockies, for France.[15] With one declaration, La Salle claimed the central portions of today's United States and hundreds of thousands of people for his King. Having accomplished a key objective, locating the mouth of the Mississippi, La Salle began his return journey northward to accomplish his other objectives. The return journey was not uneventful. The Frenchmen repulsed

---

[14] "The Minet Relation" in Weddle, Morkovsky, and Galloway, *La Salle*, 43.
[15] La Salle, "Account of the Taking Possession of Louisiana by M. De La Salle," *French Historical Collections*, I: 49.

an Indian attack and later, La Salle fell gravely ill near today's Memphis, Tennessee. Unable to travel, La Salle sent Tonti to Michilimackinac to "arrange his [La Salle's] affairs" there.[16]

Figure 15: The Mississippi River at the Gulf of Mexico as seen from the air.
Photo by the author.

Somewhere north of the Ohio River, Tonti and his group encountered a group of Iroquois warriors traveling down the Mississippi, an ominous happenstance, indeed. Although they told Tonti that a 100 more warriors would soon rendezvous with them, Tonti's group was left unharmed and allowed to continue their journey north. The group later observed several unoccupied Illinois dugouts that had been pulled from the water and left along the riverbank. Drawing closer to the vessels, Tonti's group found themselves under attack. Mistaking the French and the Indians with them for Iroquois, a large Tamaroa war party left their forest cover and charged Tonti's canoes. The Tamaroa, upon seeing the calumet that Tonti held high, quit their charge and escorted the Frenchman's group to their camp. Tonti later reported that the chiefs held a sham council to determine their fate—the Indians having already decided to burn the French. Fortunately for Tonti and the others, several other Illinois tribesmen who were among the Tamaroa, persuaded the instigators to let the French leave unharmed.[17] Continuing up the Mississippi, Tonti's party later changed course and paddled up the Illinois,

---

[16] La Salle recuperated at a small hastily built post named Fort Prudhomme, a site that is supposed to have been located near today's Memphis, Tennessee.
[17] Kellogg, *Early Narratives*, 304

eventually reaching the Des Plaines. Completing the portage to the Chicago River, Tonti retrieved the merchandise that had been buried earlier that year. He then followed the western shore of Lake Michigan, and eventually reached Michilimackinac. Until La Salle arrived at the post, Tonti would manage the explorer's business affairs there.

At his Tennessee camp, La Salle's illness began to abate; he was able to continue the trek north. Paddling up the Mississippi and then the Illinois, his party reached Starved Rock and the Illinois River rapids where the stream was so shallow that the men were forced to carry their canoes. Finding deeper water above the rapids, they arrived at a place called "the island of the rapids," presumably an island located at today's Marseilles.[18] La Salle left several men there along with ammunition for hunting. He instructed them to remain at the island until they received further orders. The explorer continued his voyage, first to his Miami post and then on to Michilimackinac. In September, a somewhat recuperated and invigorated La Salle reunited with Tonti at Michilimackinac.

While La Salle was away on his Gulf expedition, in the spring of 1682, the political climate in France had changed. La Salle's ally and protector, Frontenac, had been recalled to France. A new governor, Le Febvre de La Barre, had been appointed governor of Canada. One of La Barre's directives was to bring stability to Canada by preventing Iroquois attacks on the French, the Illinois, and other tribes. The king had also instructed La Barre to consolidate Canada's population—to discourage small settlements along the distant western rivers and lakes. La Barre was also to discourage men from leaving the settlements to trade with the Indians. These directives were given, in part, to not only thwart Iroquois attacks on unfortified settlements, but also to ensure that trade revenues went to the crown rather than to private traders. With these and other instructions, La Barre sailed for Canada.

Unchecked western expansion and illegal trade were hallmarks of the Frontenac administration. The governor also failed to protect Indian allies and Frenchmen from Iroquois attacks, even when the tribes sought the governor's protection. Moreover, by 1682, the tempestuous and haughty Frontenac had made enemies with seemingly everyone in political, religious, and business circles in New France. After several local officials protested to the French Court that Frontenac's bombastic behavior was destructive to the colony, Colbert wrote to the governor to warn him to "alter his conduct" and "principles," or face recall. But the governor refused to heed the minister's admonitions and was recalled to France.[19]

When La Barre arrived, he found the colony ill-prepared to defend itself against the powerful Iroquois; even the settlement of Montreal had no palisade.[20] Alarmed by the lack of basic security, the new governor realized that this deficit threatened Canada's very survival while British posts on Hudson Bay threatened to siphon off furs destined for France. He also learned that the Iroquois were becoming increasingly agitated with

---

[18] "The Minet Relation," in Weddle, Morkovsky, and Galloway (eds.), *La Salle*, 63.

[19] W.J. Eccles, "Buade, Louis, de, Comte de Frontenac et de Palluau," in *Dictionary of Canadian Biography*, vol. 1 (University of Toronto/Université Laval, 2003, revised 2015), accessed November 5, 2018, http://www.biographi.ca/en/bio/buade_de_frontenac_et_de_palluau_louis_de_1E.

[20] Eccles, *Canadian Frontier*, 114.

La Salle, whom they believed was arming their Illinois enemies. La Barre concluded, as apparently had the king, that the French Colony of Canada was jeopardized by defenseless towns, illegal trade, and unauthorized westward expansion, as well as personal animus by the Iroquois directed at La Salle.

In the fall of 1682, La Salle, having learned that Frontenac had been recalled, immediately took measures to win the new governor's support. He sent La Barre a letter informing the official of the status of his enterprise in the West. In the correspondence, La Salle told the governor that the Miami and Illinois were ready to relocate near a fort that he, La Salle, would build in the Illinois Country where he would parcel out land to settlers as he had done at Fort Frontenac, all privileges—La Salle reminded the governor, that he, La Salle, had been granted by royal license. La Salle included a copy of his royal patent with the letter. La Barre took La Salle's reminder as an affront to his authority. Personal provocations aside, La Barre had been instructed by the king. La Salle's venture was contrary to everything that the governor had been sent to Canada to correct.

La Barre was not going to let La Salle dictate policy. He was determined to end the explorer's operations in Illinois. Using the pretext that La Salle had not maintained the fort's defenses, La Barre seized La Salle's Fort Frontenac. La Barre wrote Minister Colbert that La Salle "has turned his back, leaving Fort Frontenac to confusion."[21] The new governor impugned La Salle's discovery of the Gulf, with the accusation that it had been "accompanied by a great deal of falsehood." Furthermore, he convinced the king that the discovery was worthless, a matter to which the monarch replied, "I am persuaded, with you, that Sieur de la Salle's discovery is very useless, and such enterprises must be prevented hereafter, as they tend only to debauch the inhabitants by the hope of gain, and to diminish the revenue from the Beaver."[22] The governor dispatched a canoe convoy, led by Olivier Morel Sieur de La Durantaye and Chevalier Louis-Henri de Baugy, to take charge of two key western forts, one at Michilimackinac, and one that would soon be built at Starved Rock.

La Barre was not La Salle's only enemy in Quebec. Canada's Intendant, Jacques Duchesneau, who understood that to keep peace between the French colonists and the Iroquois, the French had to remove any real or perceived evidence that they were arming the Illinois against the Iroquois. To this end, Duchesneau blamed La Salle for the current Iroquois unrest. He wrote the French Minister:

> The improper conduct of Sieur de la Salle... had contributed considerably to cause the latter [the Iroquois] to adopt this proceeding; for after he had obtained permission to discover the Great River of Mississippi, and had, as he alleged, the grant of the Illinois, he no longer observed any terms with the Iroquois. He ill-treated them, and avowed that he would convey arms and ammunition to the Illinois, and would die assisting them.[23]

---

[21] "Letter from M. de La Barre to Colbert," *Miami Tribal History Document Series, Great Lakes - Ohio Valley Ethnohistory Collection, Erminie Wheeler-Voegelin Archives*, Indiana University, Bloomington, and Margry, *Découvertes*, II: 303.

[22] "Louis XIV, Letter to M. de la Barre," O'Callaghan, *DCHNY*, IX: 200.

[23] M. Du Chesneau, "Memoir on the Western Indians, &c," O'Callaghan, *DCHNY*, IX: 163.

In addition to political enemies, Montreal and Quebec merchants provided more difficulties for La Salle. These men, who made their livings buying and selling furs and tanning hides delivered from the western tribes, had heavily financed La Salle's expedition with accounts that had yet to be repaid. Moreover, they believed that La Salle's discovery of the Gulf and his operations in the Illinois Country would potentially divert furs that they believed should be theirs. Coupled with La Salle's Fort Frontenac, a post that intercepted furs destined for British traders in today's New York state, and coincidentally traders in Montreal. La Salle's Gulf venture made him not only an undesirable borrower for these merchants, but also a competitor.

———————————

It is possible that, at first, La Salle had no idea that the governor had set out to destroy him. With just a few months remaining on his patent, and having achieved little, La Salle was compelled to sail to France to ask the court for an extension of his license. Before leaving for Quebec to board a ship to France, La Salle ordered Tonti to "go and collect together the French who were on the River Miami to construct the Fort of St. Louis in the Illinois."[24] Following La Salle's instructions, Tonti and his party left the Miami post and traveled back to the Illinois Country.

Tonti and his group arrived at the Marseilles Rapids where they intended to rendezvous with the men who La Salle had instructed to remain at the site. However, not all the men were there. At least one member of the group, Nicolas La Salle, no relation, had left the island and was living with a band of wintering Mascouten Indians, the severe cold having forced the French to seek refuge with the tribe. Upon learning from the Indians that Tonti had returned to the Illinois Country, the Frenchman left the Mascouten village and walked to Tonti's camp, a site that was reportedly located "in a small grove of trees" near the rapids. Tonti and the French then traveled about four leagues downstream where they established a new camp on the north side of the river, near Kaskaskia. Several days later, La Salle, who was supposed to have left for France, arrived at the French camp with two canoes of men and merchandise. He instructed Tonti and the others to cross the river and begin construction of Fort St. Louis atop Starved Rock. Until La Salle's five-year patent officially expired in May, the governor could do little to stop him.

———————————

[24] Kellogg, 304-305.

Figure 16: Today's Starved Rock, site of La Salle's Fort St. Louis.
Photo by the author.

CHAPTER FIVE
LA SALLE ILLINOIS COUNTRY HEADQUARTERS AT LE ROCHER, STARVED ROCK

Le Rocher, today's Starved Rock, is a 125-foot sandstone bluff that rises above the south bank of the Illinois River. Its summit is about 32,000 square feet, or slightly larger than two thirds of an acre. Although there are other sandstone outcrops and cliffs along this stretch of river, the Rock is by far, the most prominent, most defendable, and the most strategic—all reasons why La Salle chose Starved Rock as the site of his fort.

The Site of La Salle's Fort Saint Louis

When La Salle was in the Illinois Country in the 1680s, the Iroquois were the greatest threat to the people in the region. It was imperative, therefore, that La Salle choose a secure site for his fort, one that could be successfully defended by a handful of woodsmen.

The historic record, set down by La Salle's own hand, perfectly describes the steep faces of the bluff and the summit. La Salle wrote that the site of his fort was "on the left side of the river, on the top of a rock steep on almost every side, the foot of which is bathed by the stream so that water can be drawn from the top of the rock, which is about 600 feet in circumference. It is accessible on one side only, where the ascent is still rather steep."[1] Interestingly, the actual circumference of the summit measures approximately 657 feet.[2]

In his description of today's Lover's Leap and Eagle Cliff bluffs, La Salle wrote:

> The rocks near are all lower than that one, and the nearest is two hundred paces off, and the others further still; and between them and Fort Saint Louis a great valley extends on both sides, with a brook dividing it about the middle and flooding it when it rains. On the other side there is a meadow bordering the river in which, at the foot of the fort, there is a fine island formerly cleared by the Ilinois [sic], in which I and my settlers have sown our seed within musket shot of the fort.[3]

---

[1] "Letters of Cavalier de La Salle and Correspondence Relative to his Undertakings (1678-1685)," *Miami Tribal History Document Series, Great Lakes - Ohio Valley Ethnohistory Collection, Erminie Wheeler-Voegelin Archives* (hereafter cited as GLOVE), and Margry, *Découvertes,* II: 175.

[2] The circumference was taken via a measuring wheel on the wooden walkway that encircles the Rock's summit.

[3] The perimeter of the Lover's Leap bluff measures about 1,575 feet while nearby Eagle Cliff measures about 350 feet. "Letters of Cavalier de La Salle and Correspondence Relative to his Undertakings (1678-1685)," GLOVE and Margry, *Découvertes,* II: 176.

This passage contains more evidence demonstrating that La Salle's fort was built on Starved Rock. As described by La Salle, the Rock had a slightly higher elevation than all of the surrounding outcrops and the "great valley" divided by a brook lies between Starved Rock and Lover's Leap, which happens to be about 200 paces east. The brook is still visible today. West of the Rock is the "meadow," land that was farmed in the nineteenth-century and which today is the location of the Park's main parking lot and picnic area. At the foot of the Rock, within musket shot range, is today's Plum Island.

Figure 17: Today's Plum Island. La Salle reported that his men planted maize within musket shot range from the fort. Photo by the author.

Starved Rock's summit is nearly level, a quality unlike those of nearby Lover's Leap and Eagle Cliffs that have multi-tiered summits or hills as high as twelve feet on top of them. Starved Rock's 657-foot circumference is smaller than the 1,575-foot perimeter area of Lover's Leap, contributing to Starved Rock's easy defense even by only a small group of Frenchmen. In addition, Starved Rock defenders could see the approach of anyone, whether upstream or downstream. Defenders on Lover's Leap and Eagle Cliff bluffs would have only been afforded a clear view upstream, as Plum Island blocks the western approach to those sites. Unlike Starved Rock, the outer perimeter of Lover's Leap is riddled with ravines, cuts, and eroded areas that would have made defense of a fort on that summit, more challenging.

Fort Saint Louis

Occupying the most prominent site in the valley, the fort symbolically held France's tenuous claim to the Illinois Country. The fort not only represented France's influence in the middle of North America, the post was destined to become a trading post where the Indians would trade hides for items of European manufacture. It was also a diplomatic center, a veritable French embassy in the heart of today's America, where tribal leaders could discuss important matters concerning inter and intra tribal relations with the French. Of equal importance, Starved Rock was no longer a Native American site; it had become, in the minds of the Frenchmen at the fort, part of the French empire, under the authority of Louis XIV, the Sun King.

Perhaps the most detailed description of the fort, although the depiction may have been somewhat embellished, comes from La Salle himself. Beginning with the south or most approachable side of the Rock, the explorer wrote:

> This side is inclosed with a palisade of white oak stakes eight to ten inches in diameter and twenty-two feet high, flanked by three redoubts made of squared beams set one above another to the same height, so placed that they all protect one another. The rest of the inclosure [sic] of the rock is surrounded by a similar palisade, only fifteen feet high because it is not accessible, flanked by four other redoubts, like the others behind the palisade. There is a parapet of great trees laid lengthwise one upon another to the height of two men, with the whole filled up with earth; and the top of the palisade is a sort of cheval-de-frise, with the points tipped with iron, to prevent escalade.[4]

The walls of the fort followed the irregular shape of the Rock with the tallest and strongest defenses built on the most accessible side. There were three redoubts, square block houses used as lookouts at the flanks, which were the protruding ends or corners of the palisade or wall that surrounded the fort. To protect the most vulnerable side of the fort from musket fire from enemies atop an adjacent bluff known today as the Devil's Nose, the French built a parapet, logs piled horizontally on top of each other and bolstered by earth. Iron tips were reportedly fixed at the ends of the palisades with points set upward, to prevent attackers from scaling the walls. The rest of the fort was surrounded by palisades fifteen feet high. However, Henri Joutel, who spent the winter of 1687-1688 at Fort St. Louis, gives quite a different description of the fort's defenses. He wrote, that "the fortifications consist only of some palisades and a few houses, which are around the edge and which enclose it."[5] It is likely that La Salle, his patent waning, exaggerated the fort's appearance and potential in his correspondence with French authorities.

Inside the fort were several small buildings, including a chapel, a warehouse or magazine, living quarters, and Indian huts. The structures that extended to the edge of the cliff became the outer wall of the fort. There were also several small cabins inside the palisades, each about 20 feet square in size. One of these was owned

---

[4] Ibid. The "Frisian horse" was a medieval defensive construction consisting of a log parallel to the ground with stakes or spikes radiating out of it.
[5] Joutel in Margry, *Découvertes*, III: 494.

by d'Autray. The other cabins may have belonged to Pierre Prudhomme, the gunsmith of La Salle's expedition, and d'Autray's associates, André Hunault and Jean Filastreau. La Salle required the cabin-owners to keep a hearth and pay one *sol* of seigniorial rent every year. There was also a "corn loft" in the fort. The loft was presumably where maize grown by the French and Indians was stored for safekeeping. Not only was the corn loft used to store grain, it was also used to house the bones of an important Illinois chief who reportedly "received M. de la Salle and made a kind donation of the entire country that they [the Illinois Indians] occupied, recognizing him as their father."[6] It is possible that there may have been other structures built along the base of the Rock to store items that were too cumbersome to carry to the top of the Rock.[7]

Figure 18: A model of La Salle's Fort St. Louis at the Starved Rock State Park Visitor Center. Photo courtesy of Tom Williams.

To transport drinking water from the river and into the fort, Tonti directed his men to build what appears to have been a handle and crank system made from four large logs.[8] In order to reach the river below, a bucket tied to a rope would have been tossed outward and beyond the protruding evergreens that grew on the side of the Rock. The water-filled bucket then would have been guided by hand through the

---

[6] Ibid., 493.
[7] Henri Joutel, "Joutel's Historic Journal of Monsieur de La Salle's Last Voyage to Discover the River Mississippi," in Cox, *Journeys of La Salle*, II: 213, 217 and "Grant of La Salle to D'Autray, 1683," *Cavelier de La Salle to Jacques Bourdon d'Autray*, deed in French America Collection, Chicago History Museum Research Center.
[8] Margry, *Découvertes*, III: 494.

foliage while another person cranked a handle attached to one of the logs and thus raised it to the summit. Although Henri Joutel wrote that this water-fetching system was used as a backup and was not the primary means to collect water, La Salle wrote that the site of his fort, Starved Rock "is bathed by the stream [the Illinois River] so that water can be drawn from the top of the rock." Pierre-Francis Xavier de Charlevoix, the Jesuit traveler and writer who visited the site in 1722, remarked that anyone who attempted to get water from the river to the summit by this method "would be obliged to expose themselves [to enemy fire]."[9]

La Salle's Starved Rock fort was situated in area rich in natural resources, especially the kind utilized by the French. Coal for fueling the blacksmith's forge was abundant, as was hemp for rope, timber for building and fuel, and slate for heating. Additionally, La Salle reported that copper nuggets had been found in the valley. The fort sat high above the Illinois River, a stream that led to the Mississippi and hence the Gulf. To the east were the Forks, the confluence of the Kankakee and Des Plaines that were, after a single portage, routes to the Great Lakes. The nearby Pestikouy, today's Fox River, charts a course from southern Wisconsin, and La Salle's Aramoni, today's Vermilion River, connects Starved Rock with the rivers of today's Indiana.

The immediate area around the Starved Rock bluff would have likely been denuded of trees and brush during construction of the fort, as material to build palisades, a parapet, redoubts, and cabins and huts would have required a great deal of wood. Timber on, and immediately adjacent to Starved Rock was, as it is today, a mixed conifer and deciduous variety of which the predominant species included white and black oak, red and white cedar, white pine, as well as a smattering of red elm and ash. Because white pine and red and white cedar trees consist of a single straight trunk, with only small protruding branches that could have been easily removed with a hatchet or small ax, these species would have likely provided much of the fort's structural support. Not only because they were easier to ready for construction, but also because the typical straightness of the trunks was ideal for beams and posts. Taking advantage of the moisture-resistant quality of cedar, builders would have used cedar for the fort's roof shingles. Similarly, builders would have selected oak because of its density and strength, to construct the primary defensive fortifications, as well as for longer-lasting fuel. In addition to the use of timber for both construction and fuel, the removal of trees around the perimeter of the Rock provided protection by eliminating cover for potential enemies, should they approach the fort.

The men who lived in and around La Salle's fort had to be self-sufficient. Hundreds of miles from other European outposts, and thousands of miles from the craftsmen of Europe, these explorers and entrepreneurs survived in the Illinois wilderness by mastering a range of skills. At the time of La Salle in the Illinois Country, guns were crafted individually, fashioned from uniquely produced parts. Skilled gunsmiths who possessed the knowledge to design and fashion a lock spring that could fit a range of gun types, for example, were valuable and indispensable

9 Pierre-Francis Xavier de Charlevoix, *Journal of a Voyage to North America*, ed. Louise Phelps Kellogg (Ann Arbor: University Microfilms, 1966), II: 201.

contributors to La Salle's enterprise. In much the same way, blacksmiths repaired essential broken tools and forged hafted hatchet and axe heads. In this wilderness, men reduced lead bars to liquid shot for ammunition, grew maize for food, sawed logs for construction, and made repairs to their equipment using whatever resources were available, oftentimes, scrap.

Figure 19: Blacksmiths were important members of the French group at Fort St. Louis. Photo by the author.

With Fort St. Louis under construction, it was now time for the explorer to return to Miami Country to convince the tribe that they must now relocate near his Illinois Country post at Starved Rock.

———————

In the spring of 1681, La Salle met with Miami leaders at a St. Joseph River village, where he presented his case to them, detailing the benefits of ending their wars with the Illinois and explaining the consequences for failing to do so. La Salle's efforts were successful in convincing the Miami that peace with the Illinois would be in their best interest. That same winter, La Salle had proposed to several Illinois Indians that they take back to their village his proposed proposition that the Illinois should end their wars with the Miami. By early 1683, La Salle was ready to transform these verbal agreements into action. With the fort on the summit of the Rock under construction, the explorer planned to meet with the Miami again, this time to convince them to move to the Starved Rock area.[10]

It seems certain that since some Miami groups had agreed to settle their differences with the Illinois and join with the French, they provoked the ire of the Five Nations. The Iroquois had likely become accustomed to receiving Miami ransom, as the Miami had paid them more than 3,000 beaver pelts during the winter of 1680-1681 alone.[11] Angry that their vassals had cut off their supply of beaver and that they had agreed to ally with their Illinois enemies and their French antagonists, the Iroquois prepared to attack Miami villages during the autumn of 1682. Hearing that the Iroquois would soon strike, the Miami hastily fled their homes, even leaving without their maize, in hopes of finding sanctuary near the French. However, after learning during the winter of 1682-1683 that La Salle was headed back to what is now northwestern Indiana to meet with them, the Miami, in spite of the dangers, returned to the St. Joseph to meet with the explorer.

La Salle knew that his meeting with the Miami would have to be brief. He felt that there was a sense of urgency to these negotiations. He feared that should the Iroquois strike the Miami while he was among them, it would appear that he had directed the Iroquois against them, a situation not unlike Tonti's predicament among the Illinois two and a half years earlier.

Although the Miami had made the French king master of their beaver and their lives in 1681, the explorer could not, at this time, guarantee that the French king could protect them from the Iroquois; La Salle did not have the men or materiel to do so.[12] Only Governor La Barre, La Salle's sworn enemy, could provide those resources. The explorer had but two choices to offer the tribe: they could take their chances and remain at their villages without French support, or they could relocate near his Starved Rock fort. The Miami chiefs had no choice. They would abandon their villages and resettle in the Illinois Country.[13]

The Miami wasted little time preparing for the move. Leaving their maize and other provisions behind, they traveled as unencumbered as possible, living off the land, subsisting on whatever they could kill, catch, or gather during their flight to the upper Illinois Valley. La Salle later wrote to La Barre:

> You may judge from that, Sir, of the excellence of this country, when eight or nine hundred families, marching without any provisions, find their food everywhere, even in the neighborhood of several other villages just as populous, which take as little care as the Miamys [sp].[14]

---

[10] It appears that La Salle met with the Miami sometime in December, 1682. See Mildred Mott Wedel, "Calendar of La Salle's Travels," in *A Jean Delanglez, S.J., Anthology* (New York and London: Garland Publishing, 1985), 304.

[11] Anderson, *Relation of La Salle*, 287.

[12] Ibid., 291.

[13] "La Salle to Mons. De La Barre," GLOVE, and Margry, *Découvertes*, II: 318.

[14] Ibid.

Leaving in three groups the Miami moved, for a while, along the south shore of Lake Michigan. It appears that not long after beginning their journey, some Miami were attacked by Iroquois. La Salle reported that ten households of Miami had been killed, and in a separate incident, a Miami hunter had been ambushed and mortally wounded.[15] La Salle feared that these attacks might spark panic among the Illinois and Shawnee, tribes which might reconsider their move to the Illinois Country and their alliance with the French. Without Illinois, Miami, and Shawnee participation in the explorer's last hope to revive his trade network, his Western enterprise would vanish.

To better defend themselves against attack, the separate Miami bands consolidated into one, making a more formidable barrier for their Iroquois enemies.[16] Despite having to subsist off the land and having suffered Iroquois raids, the Miami reached the Illinois Country. They established new villages there in the spring of 1683.

Even though many Miami fled their villages for the safety of the Illinois Country, it appears that some Miami remained in what is now Indiana.[17] Since the primary reason for the Miami move was their need to escape the Iroquois, it is possible that the Miami who remained on the St. Joseph could have been bands that were on good terms with the Iroquois, having been persuaded by Allouez to join the Five Nations in an attack on the Illinois.

While La Salle was away in Miami country, Tonti oversaw the construction of Fort St. Louis. Under his direction, between eighteen and twenty-two Frenchmen felled trees, sawed logs, built structures, and erected palisades, completing the fort by March 1683.[18] Tonti then traveled west to locate the scattered Illinois bands and convince them to return to Kaskaskia. Finding at least one large Illinois settlement, Tonti plied the tribesmen with gifts in an effort to induce them to relocate at Kaskaskia. However, gifts alone were not enough to convince the Illinois to trade the safety of their western location for their old village near Starved Rock. Like that of their Miami cousins, their safety and trust that the French could protect them from the Iroquois was paramount.[19] Although no one knows what Tonti may have told or promised the Illinois, it is possible that he persuaded them to return by arguing that amicable relationships with the French, the Miami and Shawnee and living in scattered Mississippi Valley settlements left the Illinois vulnerable to attacks by the

---

[15] It is unclear exactly what La Salle meant by "households." Households could refer to family groups (five people) or could possibly mean everyone who lived in a cabin or lodge (twenty people).

[16] Margry, *Découvertes*, II: 317-319.

[17] See the 1684 Franquelin-Parkman *Carte de la Louisiane ou des voyages du Sr. De La Salle* and the 1685 Minet *Carte de la Louisiane*. It is possible that these Miami had been one of the number that allied with the Iroquois.

[18] Margry, *Découvertes,* II: 323, Nicolas La Salle in idem, I: 570 and Tonti in Kellogg, *Early Narratives,* 305. The exact number of men is difficult to determine as the two primary accounts of the number of men who went to Starved Rock to build the fort differ.

[19] Thwaites, *WHC,* XVI: 112.

powerful Sioux and other enemies.[20] Typical of Franco-Indian relations, Tonti likely offered to the Illinois easy access to French trade goods. Tonti's words were powerful and convincing. Many Illinois agreed to return to the Illinois Valley, likely arriving in the late that summer or possibly in the early fall. Once there, the Illinois men undoubtedly began to move debris left from the 1680 Iroquois destruction of the site, and after the ground had been cleared, Illinois women likely cultivated the soil, preparing it for the following year's crop.

Figure 20: A photograph of the second of two Peoria village sites that were reported by Jacques Marquette. Photo taken at the Illiniwek State Historical site in Missouri by the author.

La Salle's Indian Colony

In 1684, Jean-Baptiste Franquelin, the man credited with drawing Jolliet's maps *La Colbertie* and *La Frontenacie*, drew the now famous *Carte de la Louisiane*, which includes the lands and waterways traversed by La Salle during the years 1679 through 1682. The map was drawn in Paris based on information provided by La Salle himself, as Franquelin had never traveled west of Montreal. Franquelin's map illustrates La Salle's "Colony," a loose assemblage of Indian settlements located in the upper Illinois Valley.[21] According to the map, the colony extended approximately sixty-five miles east to west across Illinois, from today's Hennepin to somewhere

---

[20] Unlike La Salle, who could not speak Miami-Illinois in 1680, Tonti was probably able to make his point known to the Illinois chiefs in 1683 because he had likely learned some essential Miami-Illinois words and phrases while living with the tribe during the spring and summer of 1680.

[21] The reason for the term "colony" is predicated on the following: the success of La Salle's Illinois enterprise depended on the cooperation of both French and Indians; the French as "settlers," as La Salle referred to them, to cultivate the soil, and the Indians to provide hides and protection. Additionally, La Salle told Illinois chief Chassagoac in 1680 that he planned to establish a "colony" in the Illinois Country.

near Channahon, and ranged south of the Illinois River to a point near today's Aroma Park, on the Iroquois River. Bordering the outskirts of the colony to the north are villages of the Kickapoo and Mascouten.

Historians dating back to the time of Francis Parkman's 1860s classic, *La Salle and the Discovery of the Great West*, agree that 20,000 Indians left their established settlements and relocated to the Illinois Valley.[22] Historians consistently cite as evidence numbers that represent village populations illustrated on the 1684 map, and a statement by La Salle directed to French Naval Secretary Jean-Baptiste Antoine Colbert, the Marquis de Seignelay, in which the explorer claims that he "has brought together.... more than eighteen thousand" Indians to his colony.[23] Recent findings call into question whether Franquelin's map and La Salle's statement accurately represent the colony's Indian population of 1683. Is it possible that La Salle purposely exaggerated the number of Indians living in his colony for personal benefit, or have historians misinterpreted information depicted on the map? A close variant of the map, the 1685 *Carte de la Louisiane,* drawn by the explorer's engineer Minet, may provide additional insights.

The Map

To begin, Franquelin's map, the chart most often used by researchers to determine the population of La Salle's colony, is not the original; it is a nineteenth-century copy of the map; the original no longer exists. While researching his *Discovery*, Francis Parkman traveled to Paris where he met Pierre Margry, editor of the six-volume *Découvertes et établissements des Français dans l'ouest et dans le sud de l'Amérique septentrionale, 1614-1754.* It appears that it was at this time that an artist drew by hand, a copy of the map, a chart that is now in the library at Harvard University. Sometime after the map had been copied, it vanished. Without the original Franquelin map to assess accuracy, today's researchers have only the work of a copyist, one employed by two staunch defenders of La Salle. The map could be a duplicate of the original, or could contain unintended errors, or it may be biased, including information that supports La Salle regarding the location or population of Indian villages depicted on the original map.

Next to each Colony Indian village on the Parkman map are numbers that represent populations, figures that are missing on Franquelin's 1688 map of the same area. Living in today's Kankakee County are "1,300h Miamy," also mentioned by La Salle as the "Tohatchaking," and near the Forks are seen "150 Peanghichia," or

---

[22] Some of these include Temple, *Indian Villages*, 26; Alvord, *Illinois Country*, 89; and Charles J. Balesi, *The Time of the French in the Heart of North America, 1673-1818,* 4th edition (Chicago: Paginae Publication, 2014), 61.

[23] "Robert Cavalier, Sieur de La Salle, Addressed to Monseigneur de Seignelay, in the Discoveries Made by Him by Order of His Majesty Louis XIV, King of France" in *Historical Collections of Louisiana and Florida*, Second Series, edited by B.F. French (New York: Albert Mason, 1875), 4, accessed August 27, 2019, from https://archive.org/details/historicalcolle06frengoog/page/n28.

Piankashaw.[24] What does the letter "h" next to some village populations represent? Does it stand for *hommes*, "men," i.e., hunter-warriors, or could it signify *habitants,* the total number of people who lived in the village? Or is it possible that the "h" had been anglicized by the copyist and could refer to huts, Indian cabins?

The Parkman map includes the following colony population designations.

Miami groups with population numbers that include the letter "h":
- "Miamy" (Tohatchaking)...1,300h
- "Kilatica"..300h
- "Oiatenon" ("Ouiatanon" in French, "Wea" in English) 500h
- "Pepikokia"...160h

Villages that do not have the "h" next to their corresponding number:
- The "Peanghichia"(Piankashaw).................150
- The "Ilinois" at Kaskaskia............................1,200
- The "Ouabona"...70

Non-Miami-Illinois groups with a population number that includes the letter "h":
- The "Chaneunon" or Shawnee.....................700h, or possibly 200h

The 20,000 number most often cited by historians is based on the following general assumptions:
- 1 family = 1 hunter-warrior and 4 non-hunter-warriors.
- 1 fire = 2 families.
- 2 families = 10 people.
- 1 cabin = 2 fires, 4 families, 4 hunter-warriors, 16 non-hunter-warriors for a total of 20 people.[25]

If the number next to the village on the Parkman map represents hunter-warriors, whether an "h" appears next to the number or not, the colony would have been composed of roughly 4,380 hunter-warriors for a population of about 21,900 people (4,380 x 5 = 21,900). This being the case, 12,050 would have been Miami, 6,000 Illinois, 3,500 Shawnee, and 350 Ouabona. The Miami alone would comprise 55%of the colony. These numbers do not include the Miami who remained in Indiana or may have lived in Wisconsin.[26]

Minet's 1685 *Carte de la Louisiane* illustrates North American lands and waters extending from the Atlantic Ocean to the Mississippi Valley and beyond. The map also illustrates the location of Colony Indian villages, the site of Fort St. Louis, and other important geographical information.[27] Minet depicted the Piankashaw, a

---

[24] The Tohatchakingor, misspelled by La Salle, Miami subtribe were the Crane clan, while the Piankashaw means "torn ears person." Personal communication, Michael McCafferty, linguist at Indian University in Bloomington, on August 12, 2016.

[25] Zitomersky, 219. It appears that the Jesuit missionary Druillettes also used the four non-warrior to one warrior ratio for the Miami divisions.

[26] At least one Miami group appears to be living northwest of Green Bay in today's Wisconsin. See W. Vernon Kinietz, *The Indians of the Western Great Lakes, 1615-1760* (Ann Arbor: University of Michigan Press, 1965), 162.

[27] Woodbury Lowery, *The Lowery Collection, A Descriptive List of Maps of the Spanish Possessions Within the Present Limits of the United States, 1502-1820* (Washington: Government Printing Office, 1912), 165, accessed August 30, 2016 at Internet Archives at URL: https://archive.org/details/lowerycollection00lowerich.

Miami subtribe that the Parkman map locates near the Forks, as "Les Miamis." Furthermore, it is interesting that the 1,300h "Miamy" living on the Iroquois River on the Parkman map are not noted on the Minet map. Coincidentally, the Minet map neither mentions nor marks by symbol the village of the Ouabona Indians that are located on the Parkman map. Other villages, such as that of the Pepikokia found on the Parkman map, are noted by symbol, not by name. Also missing from the chart are numbers that represent estimated village populations.

Figure 21: Detail of Jean-Baptiste Franquelin's 1684 *Carte de la Louisiane* map depicting La Salle's Indian colony in present-day northern Illinois. Map courtesy of the Library of Congress. https://www.loc.gov/resource/g3300.ct000656/.

La Salle reported to Governor La Barre that between 800 and 900 families of Miami marched without provisions from their Indiana camps to their new Illinois Country settlements.[28] Taken literally, this means that a total of between 4,000 and 4,500 Miami occupying between 200 and 225 cabins moved to what is now Illinois, a number that is significantly lower than 12,050. In this same document, La Salle names four Miami subtribes: the Pepikokia, Oiatenon, Tohatchaking (or Miamy), and Kilatica, who occupied a particular position among the 800 to 900 families during their westward migration. The Oiatenon occupied the Miami rear, the position closest to the Iroquois; the Pepikokia occupied the Miami center; while the Tohatchaking and some Kilatica were reported by La Salle to have been "a long way off." Some Miamy left the 800 to 900 Miami families to pursue the Iroquois who had killed the Miami hunter, but after realizing that they might soon encounter a larger Iroquois force, they rejoined the other Miami groups. Although La Salle mentions only four Miami subtribes as included in the 800 to 900 family group that traveled to the Illinois Country, it is probable that other Miami subtribes not mentioned by the explorer were also dispersed within the Miami group.

In another correspondence La Salle wrote that the Missouri Indians and four Miami subtribes—the Piankeshaw, Kilatica, Megancockia, and the Melomelinoia— had moved to the colony and numbered between 200 and 300 fires, or between 2,000 and 3,000 people. La Salle's 800 to 900 families surely included these four Miami subtribes, as the explorer reported that at least two of them, the Pepikokia and the Kilatica, had left their Indiana villages and were among his families.[29] The Megancockia and the Melomelinoia are not depicted as living in their own villages on the Parkman map.[30] If they had moved to the Colony, they would have been living among the Miami bands noted on the map.[31]

Narrowing it down further, the Parkman map depicts the Oiatenon as settled on the north side of the Illinois River, likely in today's Bureau County. The explorer reported that they settled "to the number of thirty-five huts, are there now [near Fort St. Louis], having come away from their villages with me."[32] If one cabin equals 20 people, then 700 Oiatenon would have relocated to La Salle's colony. According to the Parkman map, the Oiatenon numbered "500h." Considering that La Salle wrote that about 700 Oiatenon were living in the colony, and the Parkman map portrays 500h of them living there, it is plausible to assume that the "h" could represent *habitants*, not *hommes*, or hunter-warriors. If this is the case, the Oiatenon

---

[28] Margry, *Découvertes*, II: 320.

[29] Ibid., II: 319-320 and II: 201.

[30] The Megancockia means "trees-which-are-large-person" and the Melomelinoia means "he tortures continuously." Michael McCafferty, linguist, personal communication, August 31, 2016.

[31] Franquelin's 1688 map of northern Illinois depicts the Megancockia living approximately forty miles north of Starved Rock. The 1688 map also shows the Kilatica living some distance up today's Fox River, not near Hennepin as illustrated on the 1684 map.

[32] La Salle in Margry, *Découvertes*, II: 202 states that thirty-five huts of Oiatenon settled in the Illinois Valley whereas La Salle in "Rivers and Natives of the Countries Explored" in GLOVE, "a hundred and twenty huts" had settled there.

population would be reduced from approximately 2,500 people, based on the assumption that 500h represents hunter-warriors only, to just 700.

Another problem surfaces when comparing the numbers representing the "Miamy" depicted on the Parkman map as 1,300h, and the Piankashaw 150 without the "h." Assuming that the 1,300h represents *habitants*, the population of the Miamy would be 1,300. If the 1,300h represents hunter-warriors, the population of the Miamy subtribe alone would be 6,500, more than the entire number of Colony Illinois Indians. If the 150 Piankashaw without the "h" are hunter-warriors, the Piankashaw would have numbered about 750. Historically, however, the Piankashaw outnumbered the Miamy prior to 1700.[33] The Parkman map does not depict the Megancockia and the Melomelinoia at all. La Salle added to the confusion when he wrote that the Missouri, Piankashaw, Kilatica, Megancockia, and Melomelinoia lived together in a single village, numbering between 2,000 and 3,000 people, and "have made their fields four leagues [roughly ten miles] from the fort." This statement by La Salle contradicts the map which indicates that 150 Piankashaw lived in their own village, approximately 44 miles east of La Salle's fort, at the forks of the Des Plaines and Kankakee Rivers, while 300h Kilatica lived in their own village south of the Big Bend, approximately 24 miles west of the fort, near Hennepin. The Missouri village is located somewhere near today's Princeton. Illinois, at least 30 miles northwest of Starved Rock. The only Miami settlement within 11 miles of Starved Rock is that of the 160h Pepikokia, near today's Ottawa, a village consisting of 160 *habitants* or a total population of only 800 if counted as hunter-warriors.

The "Kilatica" are depicted with a population of 300h. If the assumption that "h" represents *habitants* and not hunter-warriors, the Kilatica numbered 300, or if the "h" refers to hunter-warriors, 1,500.

Parkman's map shows 1,200 Illinois, without the "h," at Kaskaskia. If that number represents hunter-warriors, the village population would have been approximately 6,000, i.e., 1,200 X 5 = 6,000 (using the aforementioned four non-combatants for every warrior). Tonti wrote that the "Illinois established themselves, to the number of 300 cabins [6,000 people] near the Fort Illinois, as well as Miamis and Chawanons [Shawnee]."[34] It is unclear if the 6,000 Illinois include the Cahokia and Tamaroa, who, according to the Parkman map, lived along the Mississippi, south of its confluence with the Illinois. Minet locates only the Tamaroa in southern Illinois. But La Salle wrote that "300" huts of Tamaroa, or 6,000 people alone, had moved to his Colony.[35] This number is a gross overestimate. If the number of La Salle's Tamaroa were added to those of the Peoria, Kaskaskia, Cahokia, and other Illinois subtribes, the overall Illinois population would have been over 20,000! The Parkman map and La Salle's statement not only contradict each other, they are logically irreconcilable. Furthermore, both maps also depict the Tapouaro, the

---

[33] Michael McCafferty, *Native American Place-Names of Indiana* (Urbana: University of Illinois Press, 2008), 126.

[34] Tonti in B.F. French, *Historical Collections*, 66.

[35] "Rivers and Natives of the Countries Explored" and Margry, *Découvertes*, II: 201.

Coiracoentanon, the Moingwena, and possibly the largest of the Illinois subtribes at the time, the Peoria, living west of the Mississippi in today's Iowa. Again, both maps contradict information in La Salle's correspondences, documents that claimed that these subtribes had moved to his colony. The only possible explanation for why Tamaroa, Cahokia, Moingwena, Peoria, Tapouaro, and Coiracoentanon villages are noted on the 1684 and 1685 maps is that the maps conflate old information with new. Still it is unclear as to where these subtribes lived in 1683. Given such contradictory and inconsistent information from which to draw population estimates, it is impossible to accurately determine how many Illinois lived in La Salle's Colony in 1683. The best explanation for the contradictory information regarding the Illinois is that neither the Parkman nor the Minet map represents a single moment in time. Rather both are a hodgepodge of information collected between 1679 and 1683.

An interesting feature appears on the Minet map as it pertains to Illinois and Miami settlements. The map shows two villages immediately adjacent to each other near the approximate site of Kaskaskia. One likely explanation for the twin village symbols is that the village to the west is Kaskaskia, while the other is a village of a Miami subtribe. To this Henri Joutel wrote, "There was yet another nation, located a league and a half from said fort, called Miami, who are in a strong place, advantageous for building a strong town, being on a hill that is craggy all around, and where the river laps and passes at the foot of the rock, as it does at Fort St. Louis of the Illinois."[36] The only tall, flat, sandstone geological feature along the river located approximately one and one half leagues from Starved Rock that could have been a village site is today's Buffalo Rock. The Jesuit historian Charlevoix, who passed the bluff during his journey down the Illinois in 1721, wrote: "A league below the coal pit [at today's Ottawa] you see a rock on the right, entirely round, extremely high, and its summit in the form of a terrace; this is called the *Fort of the Miamis*, because these Indians had formerly a village there."[37]

Interestingly, the Parkman map depicts the Ouabona living north of the Illinois River and west of Fort. St. Louis. The Ouabona were not Illinois, Miami, or Shawnee, and neither were they a New England tribe. Frederick Webb Hodge's *Handbook of Indians North of Mexico* confusingly states that the Ouabona were Algonquian, "eastern"; cf. *Abnaki*. He notes that they "traded with the Spaniards, and at La Salle's solicitation, visited Fort St. Louis on Illinois r. [River] in company with the Shawnee and Chaskpe. They appear to have come from the S. [south]."[38] Linguist Michael McCafferty states that the term "Ouabona" is not Miami-Illinois at all, although the name "does suggest the Miami-Illinois term for possibly the Otoe, which is *wašoona*, which would have been written 'Ouachona' by any commonly educated Frenchman at that time [such as Franquelin]. A -ch- mistaken for a -b- is

36 Joutel in Margry, *Découvertes*, III: 481.

37 Kellogg, Charlevoix, *Journal*, II: 200.

38 Frederick Webb Hodge, ed., *Handbook of American Indians North of Mexico*, 2 parts (Washington: Government Printing Office, 1907) II: 172, accessed on August 31, 2016 at URL: https://archive.org/stream/ handbookamindians01hodgrich#page/172/mode/2up.

quite possible."[39] This seems to indicate that this group of Ouabona was the Otoe, a trans-Mississippi tribe whom La Salle referred to as the "Missouri," who, coincidentally, are not depicted on Parkman's or Minet's map. As buffalo hunters, the Otoe would have been a valuable asset to La Salle's enterprise. The Parkman map also notes the Ototanta (Otoe) living on the Des Moines River and the Missouri living along the Missouri River, while Minet's map shows only the Missouri living in today's state of the same name.[40]

One group of tribes that are conspicuously missing from both the Parkman and Minet maps are the eastern Indians, the "Moraigane," "Anhanagane," Mohegan, and the "Minissens," who had reportedly joined with La Salle. From available documents, it appears that very few of them actually lived in the colony. Henri Tonti also did not mention the northeastern tribes in his writings. One of the only references to any of these tribesmen at this time is in a letter written by Louis-Henri de Baugy, commandant of Fort St. Louis in 1684 that mentions nine Loups, or Mohegans at the fort, while the post was under siege by the Iroquois.[41]

The Shawnee are illustrated on both the Parkman and Minet maps as living along a stream, possibly, along the Vermilion River, south or west of La Salle's fort. However, the number corresponding to their population is unclear; it could be interpreted as 700h, or possibly 200h; a lack of clarity both in the numeral depicted and in the meaning of "h." It is, therefore, uncertain how many Shawnee lived in the colony.

Another important issue pertaining to the Parkman and Minet maps concerns the depicted course of the Mississippi River. La Salle was an astute observer of nature. As a Jesuit, he had studied philosophy, a broad discipline that included mathematics, geography, astronomy, and hydrography; he used that knowledge while navigating the Great Lakes and western rivers; he built a fort and began construction of a large vessel at a location where he had determined by observation, that he had passed the Illinois River rapids; he knew that he had crossed a continental divide in Michigan while traveling east in early 1680; and his geographical skills were touted by Frenchmen such as Joutel. La Salle knew how to read nature's clues regarding the courses of rivers and the topography of lands. Given his education and abilities, it appears that La Salle had intentionally misled the French Court by knowingly providing false information to the king and minister about the course of the Mississippi River, or Parkman's copyist and Minet erred in the placement of the Mississippi.

Franquelin's map, if Parkman's copyist accurately copied the original and the Minet map show the Mississippi River taking a decidedly hard turn to the west some distance below the stream's confluence with the Ohio. The maps portray the

---

[39] Michael Mc Cafferty, personal communication, August 11, 2016.

[40] La Salle calls what appears to be the Otoes, the "Missouri," a different trans-Mississippi tribe. Documents written by the explorer indicate that he was not necessarily concerned with the proper pronunciation nor locations of tribal names and oftentimes deviated from their standard spellings and usage.

[41] *Baugy to La Durantaye*, letter dated March 24, 1684, National Archives of Canada, Source RC 6515, call number MG1-Series C11A.

Mississippi flowing in a west-southwesterly course for 600 to 700 miles, through what appears to be today's states of Arkansas and Oklahoma. The river then takes a southeasterly turn and runs through what is now Texas before emptying into the Gulf. Given La Salle's skills and knowledge, a blunder of this magnitude could not be attributed to a broken compass.[42] Using the sun he could have easily determined east from west, and approximated north and south also by observing the movement of the sun. A mistake of this proportion is unimaginable unless it, as some have suggested, was intentional—a deception devised to obtain permission from the Court in his new patent to seize the silver mines in Mexico.[43] Marquette's map and *relation* made it abundantly clear that the Mississippi flows south, not west. The missionary wrote, "We had gone down to near the 33rd degree of latitude having proceeded nearly all the time in a southerly direction, when we perceived a village on The water's edge called Mitchigamea."[44] Furthermore, the Parkman map places the confluence of the Arkansas and Mississippi Rivers approximately 500 miles west of and over 250 miles north of the actual mouth of the Arkansas River, which, according to Marquette was at 33 degrees 40 minutes. The Minet map locates the juncture of the two rivers hundreds of miles to the west of its true location. The 1675 Franquelin-Jolliet *La Frontenacie* map also shows the Mississippi River coursing in a southerly direction, on an approximate angle of two-degrees to the west between the confluence of the Ohio and the Mississippi and the juncture of the Arkansas and Mississippi. If the explorer provided Franquelin and Minet, two men with no first-hand knowledge of the course of the Mississippi, false information regarding the course of the river, is it not possible then that La Salle might exaggerate the population of his colony?

The Parkman and Minet maps are not reliable sources.[45] They appear to be collages assembled using information gleaned during La Salle's travels between 1679 and 1682. La Salle's correspondences provide another account about the tribes who had relocated to his Colony in 1683. It is unclear and unverifiable whether Parkman's copyist accurately reproduced Franquelin's original map, and it is uncertain what the "h" next to some numbers represents. Tribes and subtribes reported by La Salle as having moved to his colony are not depicted on the two maps; meanwhile, other Colony tribes are shown living hundreds of miles away. Numerous statements by La Salle directly contradict information illustrated on the maps. For these and for other reasons, Parkman or Minet maps provide limited usefulness to researchers in the study of the tribes and their numbers at La Salle's colony in 1683.

---

[42] In early 1682, addressed in chapter four
[43] "Petition of La Salle, Addressed to Monseigneur de Seignelay" in E. B. Osler, *La Salle* (Canada: Longman, 1967), 160-161.
[44] Marquette in Thwaites, *Jesuit Relations*, 59: 149.
[45] And neither do any of the Franquelin variant maps.

Statements by La Salle

Knowing that his patent would soon expire and that he would need more time to accomplish his original goals, La Salle was forced to travel to France to plea for an extension. His voyage to France in 1683 was for one purpose only: to obtain royal approval to complete his unfinished Western enterprise in the Americas. By 1683, he planned to have established commercial alliances with the western tribes, to have a functioning post on the Gulf, and to have paid off his many creditors who were now demanding repayment. He had no means to supply the tribes with the goods that he promised them, he had few guns and little powder to defend the Colony, and he had no resources for assistance. Before any of these goals could be accomplished, La Salle had to obtain a new patent from the king.

In the spring of 1684, La Salle met with the Marquis de Seignelay, son of the late French Controller General of Finance and Minister of the Marine Jean-Baptiste Colbert. La Salle pleaded his case to Seignelay, who, in turn, presented La Salle's petition to the king. In his memorandum to the marquis, La Salle wrote that he hoped,

> *Monseigneur* will be pleased to continue in the title and government of the fort which he has erected in the country of his discovery, where he has placed several French settlers, and has brought together many savage nations, amounting to more than eighteen thousand in number, who have built houses there, and sown much ground, to commence a powerful colony.

The explorer intended this statement to be corroborated by Franquelin's new map.

La Salle had to build a strong case for himself if he were to be successful in obtaining a new patent. All information including numbers of tribes and tribesmen, and locations of forts and Indian settlements, and past statements by royal authorities would need to support his narrative, and any potential benefit to the Church, country, or king must be exploited. By claiming that 18,000 Indians had settled in the Illinois Valley, and that he had "placed" French settlers near his fort, implied that the settlers were farmers and not *coureurs de bois*; La Salle was portraying this collection of tribes and Frenchmen as the foundation of a permanent, self-sufficient French colony. His colony was also located along primary water arteries that flowed into the Gulf of Mexico, where the explorer had planned to establish a year-round port. These 18,000 Indians would become potential converts to Catholicism and as French influence and French civilization spread among the regional tribes, the Indians would become loyal French confederates. La Salle also reported that some Indian children had been given to him "to be brought up in the French manner." He would train these young people to become "interpreters, and for making peace."[46]

More importantly, 18,000 Indians meant that La Salle could potentially muster about 3,600 warriors to defend the Colony against the formidable Iroquois $(18,000 \div 5 = 3,600)$. By way of comparison, La Salle's 3,600 warriors would

---

[46] "Rivers and Natives of the Countries Explored" in *Miami Tribal History Document Series, GLOVE*, and Margry, *Découvertes*, II: 201.

outnumber the army that Canada Governor Denonville would assemble to strike the Iroquois homeland in 1687.[47] These same warriors would provide hides needed to operate the explorer's Western enterprise and provide capital to satisfy La Salle's many creditors. Finally, if necessary, these warriors could be gathered in short notice and dispatched to the Gulf in case hostilities stemming from Spain's recent declaration of war against France were to break out.

La Salle's own correspondence demonstrates that he was prone to exaggeration, both positive and negative. For example, he exaggerated potential hazards in Lakes Erie, Huron, and Michigan; he overplayed the importance of the Ohio River over the Illinois; he disparaged the Chicago harbor and the fertility of Illinois lands; and he complained about the scarcity of bison in the Illinois Country. We have also seen how he exaggerated the number of Tamaroa that moved to his Illinois Colony, "300" huts of them, or 6,000 people alone. La Salle's depiction of Fort St. Louis' formidability is in stark contrast to that of Henri Joutel, who reported that "the fortifications consist only of some palisades and a few houses, which are around the edge and which enclose it."[48]

In short, La Salle controlled all information regarding everything that occurred in western North America. No one, priest, *voyageur*, or government official could dispute his numbers, his descriptions, or his observations. While some Canadian authorities committed to thwarting La Salle's enterprise wrote unflattering and accusatory letters to the king and minister, these letters were based on hearsay, rumor, and innuendo—not personal observation or direct knowledge. If La Salle reported that 18,000 Indians lived in his Colony, the best Canadian officials could not counter his claims. Instead, they would accuse La Salle of provoking the Iroquois, failing to maintain Fort Frontenac, or declare that the explorer's discoveries were useless.[49] La Salle had everything to gain by crafting his narrative and manipulating claims including the description of tribes, and numbers associated with the Illinois Country.

It is impossible to know the Indian population of the Upper Illinois Valley in 1683. Contradictory statements, inflated numbers, political and economic intrigue, mysterious markings copied from lost maps, differing calculation methods, and falsehoods cloud any reasonable attempt to draw conclusions about the numbers of tribesmen and the location of their Illinois Country villages. Limited speculations based on rough estimates are the best information available. Perhaps 20,000 Indians did live in the colony, but before that number can accepted, many unanswered questions remain, and much irreconcilable information must be

---

[47] Denonville's famous Iroquois campaign mustered 2932 men into French service (1,632 regulars, over 900 Canadian militia, and about 400 Indian allies). See W. J. Eccles, "Brisay de Denonville, Jacques-René de, Marquis de Denonville," in *Dictionary of Canadian Biography* (Canada: University of Toronto/Université Laval, 2003), II: 98-104.

[48] Margry, *Découvertes*, III: 494.

[49] M. Du Chesneau, "Memoir on the Western Indians, &c," O'Callaghan, *DCHNY*, IX: 163; "Letter from M. de La Barre to Colbert," Margry, *Découvertes*, II: 303.

reconciled. Rather than accept what previous population estimates based on faulty assumptions and conflicting data have concluded, it is better to recognize that the number of Indians who lived in La Salle's Colony in 1683, may never be known with certainty.

Land Grants

With his fort built and the tribes moving to his colony, La Salle now had a number of obligations to fulfill if his enterprise based on intertribal relations and large-scale Franco-Native American trade were to become a success. Not only did La Salle have to provide trade goods for thousands of Indians, to keep peace between the Illinois and Miami, he also had to intervene, when necessary, in their intertribal squabbles, and festering old disputes and rivalries. It was also La Salle's responsibility to act as a liaison between all the Indians and the French, to ensure that relations between his men and the tribes remained cordial. Equally significant, La Salle was responsible for all administrative decisions that affected the tribes and the French.

One aspect of that administrative responsibility was La Salle's authority to award land grants. La Salle elected to use this power to his advantage. The explorer had already communicated his intentions to parcel out land for settlement to La Barre, to several men whom, La Salle claimed, "have asked for them."[50] These land grants would make it difficult to extract La Salle and his settlers from the Illinois Country since he had royal authority to award grants of land. La Barre likely had no authority to revoke legally awarded land grants. Remaining in the Illinois Country would compel the governor to dispatch a courier or military officer to deliver orders for La Salle to report to Quebec. This delay would provide the explorer with a few extra months of time to maneuver his enterprise into a position more favorable to him, thereby strengthening his position in seeking an extension of his patent with the French Court. By awarding land to settlers, La Salle would take the first steps in the colonization of the Illinois Country.[51] While the explorer remained in the West, unbeknownst to him, the officer bearing the orders for La Salle to report to Quebec was en route to Starved Rock.

La Salle's first land grant was awarded to Jacques Bourdon d'Autray "in recognition of his service which he has performed as well in the discovery of Louisiana as in the construction of Fort St. Louis where he has served well and has done his duty and honor."[52] D'Autray was a Canadian nobleman and son of the first *procureur général* of Quebec. He entered La Salle's service in 1675 and remained a loyal partisan until the explorer's death. The services he performed for La Salle in

---

[50] La Salle in Margry, *Découvertes*, 287-301.

[51] La Salle's royal patent gave him the same authority, including the power to grant land, on "the same terms and conditions as Fort Frontenac." See "Letters Patent," in French, *Historical Collections*, I: 35.

[52] Jacques Burdon Sieur d'Autray was a Canadian nobleman and son of the first Procureur General of Quebec. He joined La Salle in 1675 and accompanied the explorer between 1679 and 1683. In 1687 d'Autray and Tonti joined Denonville's Iroquois campaign. D'Autray was killed by Iroquois in 1688 while he was en route to Montreal from Fort Frontenac. Pease and Werner, *French Foundations*, 19.

the discovery of Louisiana included accompanying the explorer through the Great Lakes and into the Illinois Country in 1679-80, making the long winter trek from Fort de Crèvecoeur as far as the French post at Niagara, returning to the Illinois Country with La Salle later that year to search for Tonti, spending three winter months on an island in the Des Plaines River guarding La Salle's merchandise, accompanying the explorer down the Mississippi and leading one of the three exploratory parties that reached the Gulf.[53] D'Autray was also a key figure in the construction of La Salle's Fort St. Louis.[54] Unlike other Frenchmen in La Salle's employ, the explorer could trust d'Autray to do as he had been instructed and to faithfully complete any assignment given to him.

D'Autray's grant stretched 126 linear arpents along the south shore of the Illinois River and forty-two arpents deep.[55] In today's terms, the grant was about 4.57 miles long by 1.525 miles wide. D'Autray and his successors were allowed to hunt and fish on the land and river, build a church and a mill, and trade with the Indians. He was required to keep 300 square arpents "in forest trees of full growth." Other stipulations gave him "rights of dovecote, of wine press, of fortifications, and of low justice."

According to d'Autray's deed, the grant stretched from "the brook besides which we wintered" upstream including the, "island [possibly today's Leopold's Island] which is in the middle of the aforesaid river of the Illinois above the beginning of the great rock [Starved Rock] which the river bathes on the north side about one league above the aforesaid brook."[56] The question is: where is the brook that La Salle and d'Autray had wintered?

The boundaries of d'Autray's land grant and the location of "the brook" are found in the earlier account of La Salle's travels. In December 1680 La Salle concealed his goods and supplies in a rock hollow, or crevice, just before he and his men traveled downstream to search for Tonti. The explorer also stationed three men on an island near the rock-hollow to "keep a sharp lookout" on the goods. Failing to locate his missing lieutenant, La Salle and his group returned to the rock hollow to retrieve their goods and supplies. With the temperatures plummeting, the Illinois River began to freeze, requiring the French to build sledges to haul their goods up the Illinois River and out of the Starved Rock area. La Salle reported that he and his men spent 18 days building sledges. This time was most likely spent at a site only a few yards away from the rock hollow where he had hidden his goods and supplies. The only noteworthy rock-hollow adjacent to this stretch of river is located at the end of a large geological feature known today as Little Rock, an obtrusive rock

[53] It is uncertain whether or not d'Autray arrived at Fort Frontenac with La Salle. He may have remained at Niagara to recuperate from sickness he from which suffered during the long journey while the explorer continued to Fort Frontenac with "three fresh men." See *Relations of La Salle*, 167-169.

[54] La Salle, Pease and Werner, *French Foundations*, 19.

[55] In 1683, a French arpent was both a linear and square measurement. In length, an arpent is 58.47 meters or 191.835 feet long. In area, an arpent is about 0.845 of an acre.

[56] *Cavelier de La Salle to Jacques Bourdon d'Autray*, deed in the French America Collection, Chicago History Museum Research Center and Pease and Werner, 20.

formation that also includes a large rock shelter, which is next to a *ruisseau* or stream.

Figure 22: The sandstone promontory known as the Little Rock.
The most likely location of the site where the French hid goods and supplies in a crevice or rock hollow while La Salle and the others searched for Tonti in December 1680. Photo by the author.

These 18 days are the only recorded time that La Salle and d'Autray camped during the winter, at any place in the Starved Rock area, during any of their travels together, before the construction of Fort Saint Louis. Nineteenth-century maps also reveal that a small island was once located in the river approximately 100 yards west of Little Rock.[57] From this location, the three men stationed there by La Salle, could have watched the cache of items from the island's "eastern point," exactly where the explorer instructed them to conceal themselves.[58] The stream that flows next to the Little Rock site is the only one on the south side of the river that flows directly into the Illinois; all other brooks and streams empty into ancient paleo-channels that lie between the Illinois River and the canyons from which they emanate. The paleo-channel on the south side of the Illinois River is now, and has been for many centuries, just a series of long, narrow, and swampy depressions.

---

[57] See Woerrman Maps, slide 22
[58] Anderson, *Relation of La Salle*, 229.

Figure 23: One of paleo-channels located between bluffs at Starved Rock State Park and the Illinois River. Streams that emanate from above the cliffs between Starved Rock and the Little Rock site flow into ancient paleo-channels and do not flow directly into the Illinois River.
Photo by the author.

The Little Rock site is the only place in the entire Starved Rock area where a "brook" is located next to a rock hollow and rock shelter, on the south shore of the river, and adjacent to an island that is within the boundaries of d'Autray's land grant.[59]

The location of d'Autray's land grant is significant, not only because it was the first land grant in today's Illinois, and that it was the first tiny step to the eventual expulsion of the Native Americans from the Prairie State, but also because the site of the grant fit into La Salle's greater vision of a transcontinental system of trade and commerce. Located at the far end of the Starved Rock rapids, La Salle planned that hides and pelts traded at Fort St. Louis would be carried a short distance down the Illinois River to Little Rock, where d'Autray's land grant commenced. From there, the commodities would be either stored for safekeeping, or loaded onto large vessels, like the 42-foot bark the explorer's men began building at Fort de Crèvecoeur. From Little Rock, the peltry would be transported down the Illinois and Mississippi Rivers

---

[59] In 1992, Illinois Conservation Police Officers arrested a Homewood, Illinois man for illegally collecting artifacts on state properties. Located among the horde of seized items was a French gun spall consistent with muskets used during the La Salle period. The spall was illegally taken from the Little Rock site.

to the Gulf. About this arrangement, the explorer wrote that the "ships of the said company" [La Salle's company] would "arrive by the river Colbert" where hides that d'Autray collected [below the Illinois River rapids] would be transported to the "storehouse which shall be established at the mouth of the said river."[60] La Salle also wrote that his men at the Starved Rock fort, "shall be constantly preparing what is necessary for loading the first ships which come from France, in order to avoid unnecessary expenses on the first voyage, and the provisions necessary for the maintenance of the colony to be established on the Great River, near the sea, for the first year."[61] It is clear that not only did La Salle hope to take hides traded at Fort St. Louis down the Illinois River and to the Gulf; but he also planned to construct a vessel in order to do so. He also knew that by designating the land grant boundaries, d'Autray's land began at the end of the rapids and it would be from there that barks would be loaded and sent downstream. Moreover, it is likely, that La Salle understood that the melting snow and spring rains that annually inundate the river in March and April, when the tribes are returning to their summer villages from the winter hunt, and, coincidentally, when trade is conducted, would make the shallow and rocky waters of the Illinois below Starved Rock navigable in order to carry hides to the Little Rock site.

In August 1683, nearly three months after his royal license had expired, La Salle awarded a second land grant, this one to Pierre Prudhomme, La Salle's gunsmith, who, like d'Autray, was an important member of the 1682 Gulf expedition. As gunsmith, or armorer, Prudhomme could, if necessary, craft gun parts from seemingly useless bits of metal and could forge nails and other items from salvaged materials. La Salle's success depended on Prudhomme's ability to keep the guns firing, the knives and hatchets operable, and the tools in good condition. His talents were also vital during the construction of Fort St. Louis. Prudhomme's land began "four arpents to the west of the brook or ravine which one first comes to on the right-hand side in descending the river of the Illinois from the little river named Aramoni [Vermilion]," or, the grant began about 256 yards west of the mouth of the Little Vermilion River. The grant extended for 44 arpents (1.59 miles) in length by 44 in depth.[62] Today, part of Prudhomme's land is within the city limits of La Salle, Illinois. Like d'Autray's grant, the property was under title of fief and seigniory. Under this system, men such as d'Autray and Prudhomme owned the property much like a medieval lord or knight. Like the feudal system in France and Canada at this time, both men had the option to parcel the property to others under the conditions set by La Salle.

It appears that La Salle may have awarded other Frenchmen grants of land near his fort, including men known only as Messieurs Laurriet and Brossard, who La Salle described as "inhabitants *near* Fort Saint Louis" (emphasis added). Reliable documents that contain the names of other land grantees and the locations of their

---

[60] "Grant of La Salle to D'Autray, 1683," Pease and Werner, *French Foundations*, 20.
[61] "La Salle to a Friend" in *Miami Tribal History Document Series*, GLOVE, and Margry, *Découvertes*, II: 301.
[62] "Grant of La Salle to Prudhomme," Pease and Werner, *French Foundations*, 28-29.

properties have been lost to history. It is possible that Nicolas Doyon, André Hunault, and Jean Filastreau, men known as "assigns," in the language of the d'Autry's deed, may have been living on d'Autry's land, outside the fort.[63]

By 1687, some of the French who had received grants of land from La Salle near Starved Rock would become a matter of consternation for Canada's Governor Denonville, who wrote to minister Seignelay:

> M. de la Salle has made grants at Fort St Louis to several Frenchmen who reside there since many years without desiring to return. This has given rise to infinite disorders and abominations. Those to whom M. de la Salle has given grants are all young men without any means of cultivating the soil; every 8 days they marry Squaws after the Indian fashion of that country, whom they purchase from the parents at the expense of the merchants. Those fellows pretending to be independent and masters on their distant lands, every thing is in disorder. This year 10 plotted to go off to the English, and conduct them to the Micissipy.[64]

La Salle planned to stay in the Illinois Country to guide his fledgling Colony, thereby embedding and consolidating his claims in the Illinois, and, in remaining at the Rock, La Salle hoped to avoid meeting La Barre, a man so vengeful that he wanted to see La Salle dead.[65] By this time, he had planned to have his Starved Rock fort fully stocked with trade goods. Because the fort had only been completed two months earlier, however, the trade system was not yet functional. As a result, La Salle's small pool of trade goods diminished quickly. His many setbacks during the previous five years had made his overall plans impossible to accomplish within the time constraints of his license.

La Salle also recognized the need to defend his Colony from the Iroquois threat. Safety in numbers was important but without adequate weapons and an ample supply of ammunition, defending against the powerful Iroquois would be difficult. His 20 Frenchmen at the Starved Rock fort needed ammunition. To replenish their dwindling supply, La Salle sent two of his Starved Rock "settlers" to Canada to procure more. The settlers carried a letter, addressed to La Barre, petitioning the governor to allow the men to return with the ammunition to the Illinois Country.[66] With La Salle's patent now expired, the vindictive governor seized the opportunity to thwart his rival's plans and ambitions. La Barre detained La Salle's two men, thus, preventing them from returning with the needed supply. La Salle resigned himself to the fact that he had to journey to Quebec, and then to France, to secure permission to continue his work.[67]

---

[63] Ibid., 20, 24, "La Salle to the People of Fort St. Louis,"; "M. de Denonville to M. de Seignelay," O'Callaghan, *DCHNY*, IX: 344-345.

[64] "M. de Denonville to M. de Seignelay," O'Callaghan, *DCHNY*, IX: 344-345.

[65] "Remonstrance of Sieur de la Salle against M. de la Barre's Seizure of Fort Frontenac," O'Callaghan, *DCHNY*, IX: 215.

[66] La Salle in Margry, *Découvertes,* II: 317.

[67] La Salle's June 4, 1683 letter to La Barre (ibid., 317-328) written from the Chicago portage, requested that La Barre allow two of his "settlers" from *this* fort to procure ammunition to defend against the powerful Iroquois and the Panimaha, and return to the Illinois Country. Some historians

La Salle left Starved Rock in the company of three Frenchmen—Barbier, Nicolas La Salle, and young L'Esperance—and two Shawnee Indians in late August of 1683, placing Tonti in charge of his fort during his absence.[68] Somewhere on their journey, between the Forks and the Chicago portage, La Salle's party encountered several canoes that were headed to Fort Saint Louis. The canoes were commanded by Louis-Henri Baugy, who had been instructed by the governor to arrest illegal traders whom he might encounter in the Lakes, take possession of and assume command at Fort Saint Louis, and, if Baugy determined that any of La Salle's possessions at the fort had been illegally or improperly obtained, he was to seize the property. In a letter that Baugy delivered to the explorer, La Salle was ordered to report as soon as possible to the governor at Quebec, a meaningless directive in that La Salle was en route. While La Salle had anticipated the governor's actions, he nonetheless likely recoiled from the scope and personal implications of this reality.

It was at this time that La Salle scribbled a letter to "the inhabitants near Fort Saint Louis in Louisiana" (Louisiana was another name for the lands La Salle claimed in 1682 and for the Illinois Country). La Salle assured his settlers that the change in command at the fort and the problems caused by the colonial administration in Canada were only a "little storm" to be averted. La Salle, a man whose word was respected, told his people that even though there were few trade goods or supplies then at the fort, he would purchase more goods, even at full price at Michilimackinac, and that the goods would be sent to his traders at Starved Rock to be sold at half price. La Salle intentionally planned to take a financial loss in order to keep the tribes supplied, and to fulfill the promises he had previously made to the Colony Indians and his men. He exhorted his people to work "in security" since their profit and that of La Salle, depended on the Illinois Country settlement. Assuring the men that the goods would arrive by autumn 1684, he wrote, "you shall have goods according to your needs, and perhaps something to drink to my health, since I have learned that Rolland is keeping a barrel of brandy for me."[69] La Salle also instructed the people at Fort Saint Louis to "get together as many buffalo skins as you can," a directive that emphasized compliance with the restrictions detailed in his royal patent. La Salle further implored his men to accept Baugy and to "do nothing which looks like plot or party." He told his people, "You will gain by obeying and lose by murmuring." Finally, he requested that they live "in harmony and cherish for

---

believe that *this* fort was a post located at the Chicago portage. The fort to which La Salle refers is not a tiny, insignificant post at Chicago, but his Illinois Country headquarters at Starved Rock where he had previously awarded land grants to several Frenchmen. It is unlikely that the powerful Iroquois would travel over 700 miles from Upstate New York to attack a diminutive post at Chicago. (Emphasis added.)

[68] Weddle, Morkovsky, and Galloway, *Minet Relation*, 64. It appears that there were between 18 and 22 men at Starved Rock when construction of the fort commenced (see footnote 1 above). La Salle sent two to Canada to procure ammunition. Three French and two Indians accompanied him to Canada in August 1683, leaving Tonti with between 13 and 17 men. See "La Salle to the People of Fort Saint Louis," Pease and Werner, *French Foundations*, 37.

[69] It is possible that Rolland was in fact Francois Lenoir, a merchant of Lachine. Pease and Werner, *French Foundations,* 37, fn. 1.

Monsieur Tonti the gratitude demanded by the generosity with which he serves my interests and yours."[70] La Salle handed the letter to Baugy who continued his journey to Fort St. Louis; La Salle's party resumed their trek upstream.

The exact number of canoes in Baugy's party, or the number of men in the party is uncertain, though it is likely that Baugy's group was relatively small. According to La Salle, during the spring of 1683, La Barre had sent "more than thirty canoes loaded with goods" to Fort Saint Louis led by Baugy, Olivier Morel La Durantaye, and Daniel Greysolon Du Lhut.[71] The written historical record, however, indicates that only Baugy's party, the smallest of the three French groups, actually arrived at Fort Saint Louis. According to Jesuit Father Enjalran, writing to Governor La Barre from Michilimackinac in late August 1683, Baugy's party paddled through the strategic Straits of Mackinac and continued south along the eastern shore of Lake Michigan, in order to intercept La Salle, should the explorer take that route to Canada.[72] La Durantaye's party, likely the largest of the three groups as he was assigned to command the important French post at Michilimackinac, passed through the Straits and followed the western shore of the lake to Green Bay, where his party attempted to restore order among the unruly Potawatomi. After accomplishing little at the bay, he and his soldiers and *voyageurs* returned to the Michilimackinac fort.[73] Du Lhut's party, according to Enjalran, after separating from La Durantaye, arrived at Green Bay sometime after La Durantaye had left the bay area. Arriving at the "head of the Bay," Du Lhut's men unloaded their heavy cargo of trade goods and supplies at the St. Francis Mission and then proceeded up the Fox River in a "warlike array" to inform the Potawatomi "of the resentment felt by the new Onontio [La Barre] on account of their past assassinations and the bad feelings they display toward the French," and the tribe's "inspiring the other nations with their own hostile spirit." After reportedly clearing the route up the Fox River, Du Lhut's men fetched the goods that they had stored at the mission and headed to Nadouessis [Sioux] country, presumably in today's southern Minnesota, where he and over thirty men traded with the tribe.[74]

After La Salle and Baugy parted company, the explorer continued his trek to Quebec. Along the way he reportedly saw many canoes heading west, some of them allegedly so loaded with merchandise that the *voyageurs* in them had little room for food and provisions. Although the explorer had no way to verify his claim, La Salle later protested that it was "publicly known," that La Barre's men at Fort Frontenac had sent out more than 100 canoes loaded with trade goods; remarkably, that number would have represented 75 more trade canoes than the King had allowed La

---

70 "La Salle to the People of Fort St. Louis, Sept. 1, 1683," Ibid., 41.

71 Remonstrance of Sieur de la Salle against M. de la Barre's Seizure of Fort Frontenac," O'Callaghan, *DCHNY*, IX: 215.

72 "Letter of Father Enjalran to Lefevre de la Barre," 1683 in Thwaites, *WHC*, XVI: 110-111.

73 Ibid. and Bernard Weilbrenner, "Morel de La Durantaye, Oliver," in *Dictionary of Canadian Biography*, vol. II (Toronto: University of Toronto Press, 1969), 488-489.

74 See "Letter of Father Enjalran to Lefevre de la Barre," 1683 in Thwaites, *WHC*, XVI: 110-111 and "Remonstrance of Sieur de la Salle against M. de la Barre's Seizure of Fort Frontenac" in O'Callaghan, *DCHNY*, IX: 213-216.

Salle, to send west.[75] These canoes, however, were not all en route to Starved Rock; their destinations were to all parts of the West, including the Sault, Mackinac, Green Bay, and Sioux Country, with the remaining few, to Starved Rock.[76] Furthermore, in March 1684, 200 Iroquois besieged Fort St. Louis for six days while the colony tribes were away during their winter hunt. During the siege, Baugy wrote to La Durante at Michilimackinac that there were only twenty-four Frenchmen at the fort. Since only between 18 and 22 men were at the Rock during construction of the Staved Rock fort, that two men had been sent to Canada to fetch supplies and ammunition, and that La Salle had left Starved Rock with three French and two Indians, Baugy's party would have had to have been small, perhaps consisting of only a mere handful of men.[77]

La Salle arrived in Quebec where he boarded a vessel bound for France. Arriving there, he petitioned the French Court for an extension of his expired patent. Rather than sail to Quebec and paddle the long series of rivers and lakes to reach the mouth of the Mississippi, La Salle, instead planned to sail directly to the Gulf to reach the Great River, establish a French colony, and build his port. After considering the benefits to the Church and France, the satisfied king granted La Salle permission to resume and expand his western enterprise.

A new expedition was organized. It sailed to the Mississippi by way of the Gulf. Serious setbacks plagued this expedition to such an extent that those of the first expedition seemed relatively insignificant. In the Caribbean, one of La Salle's vessels was captured by Spanish privateers. Later, the other vessels, having missed the mouth of the Mississippi, anchored 400 miles to the west of it, at Matagorda Bay, Texas, where one of his two supply ships, *l'Aimable,* was lost in Cavallo Pass. Living in inhospitable conditions, and suffering through the many confrontations with La Salle, Indians, and each other, many of the French settlers and nearly all the soldiers of this expedition, returned to France aboard the fleet's battleship escort, the *Joly.* Those who remained built a permanent settlement on the Texas mainland (another Fort St. Louis), only to be confronted with further difficulties when the *La Belle,* the only remaining supply ship and the last link to Europe, was lost on Matagorda Bay.[78] La Salle and his colonists were stranded in an unforgiving and foreign land, surrounded by hostile Karankawa Indians. La Salle's only option was to secure assistance at the closest French outpost, Fort St. Louis on Starved Rock, nearly 1,300

---

[75] An observation noted by La Salle in ibid., 214. La Salle was prohibited from dispatching more than 25 canoes. Historian Charles Balesi wrote that under La Barre's watch there were as many as 200 Frenchmen at the Rock in 1683. Balesi, *Time of the French,* 71.

[76] "Remonstrance of Sieur de la Salle against M. de la Barre's Seizure of Fort Frontenac" in O'Callaghan, *DCHNY,* IX: 214.

[77] National Archives of Canada, RC 6515, call number MG1-Series C11A. Translation from a copy of the original by Michael McCafferty of Indiana University.

[78] La Salle's ship *La Belle* ran aground about a quarter mile from shore on the southern end of Matagorda Bay. In the 1990s, the ship was located and archaeologists excavated the vessel after building a coffer dam around the site. See James E. Bruseth and Toni S. Turner, *From a Watery Grave, the Discovery and Excavation of La Salle's Shipwreck, La Belle* (College Station: Texas A&M University Press, 2005), 3, 25, 26.

miles away. In early 1687, La Salle with a group of Frenchmen began the difficult trek to the distant Illinois Country. During the long journey through the Texas wilds, disputes erupted among party members. In time, some of the disgruntled men turned their anger on him, conspiring to murder their leader.[79] Somewhere near today's Navasota, Texas, the men ambushed and killed La Salle.[80] The conspirators stole his clothing, and abandoned his body.

La Salle was dead. For a while, it appeared that with his death, a dream also died, the dream of establishing an intra-continental trade empire via the Atlantic and the Gulf, thus opening the southern door to the continent's inland waterways. Fate had other ideas, however. Even though the architect was gone, his ideas lived on, becoming realized in the nineteenth and twentieth-centuries.

---

[79] The conspirators included men named Duhaut, Heins, l'Archeveque, and Liotot.

[80] Henri Joutel was the primary chronicler of the failed La Salle expedition. See "Journal of Monsieur de La Salle's Last Voyage," Cox, *Journeys*, II: 124-127. Although many historians assumed that the site of La Salle's murder was the Trinity River in Texas, a reassessment of the written record indicates that the site was likely along the Brazos River. See Henri Joutel, *The La Salle Expedition to Texas: The Journal of Henri Joutel, 1684-1687*, ed. William C. Foster (Austin: Texas State Historical Association, 1998), 33.

CHAPTER SIX
LA SALLE'S ILLINOIS COUNTRY LEGACY

When Baugy arrived at the Rock, he removed Tonti from command and usurped that authority himself. Baugy would remain in charge at Fort St. Louis until late spring of 1685, when Tonti would be reinstated by the king. Tonti and his two associates, François Boisrondel and the Sieur de Bellefontaine, managed La Salle's business affairs in the west while La Forêt managed La Salle's business affairs from Montreal and at Fort Frontenac.[1] Tonti worked to keep peace among the Colony tribes, paddled to the Gulf hoping to locate La Salle, and later recruited and organized a Franco-colony Indian contingent to march against the Iroquois. La Forêt purchased trade goods and supplies, hired experienced traders, laborers, and a surgeon to work at the Rock, and hired *voyageurs* to transport merchandise west in the fall and furs east in the spring.[2]

Unlike La Salle, Tonti, La Forêt, and their traders were allowed to trade, not only in bison hides, but they were also free to barter for pelts of fur-bearing animals including beaver and otter. La Salle's patent had placed strict prohibitions on the type of peltry he could purchase, preventing him from trading anything other than bison hides.

After Tonti and La Forêt learned of La Salle's death, La Forêt sailed to France to petition the Court for La Salle's Illinois trade concession, an enterprise in which both men were heavily invested. In 1690, the request was granted and they became the new proprietors of the Illinois trade. By this time, however, the alliances that La Salle had worked so assiduously to establish and one that Tonti had worked diligently to maintain, were rapidly dissolving. By 1689, nearly all the non-Illinois tribes had left the Starved Rock area, many of them returning to their former lands, while it appears that some Miami established camps in today's Chicago area. In the fall of 1691, the Illinois abandoned Kaskaskia and reestablished new villages at Lake Peoria, leaving the French with little choice but to move with the tribe. For the decade following the French and Native American abandonment of the Starved Rock area, Lake Peoria would become the center of French trade and occupation in the Illinois Country.

The Legacy

It is important to note that comparatively little trade was conducted at Fort St. Louis during La Salle's time in the Illinois Country, most of it being exchanges of good will intermingled with small gestures of friendship. With his license expired and his inability to acquire trade goods in Canada, La Salle's commercial operations were

---

[1] La Forêt traveled to Starved Rock in late 1686 before heading east to join Governor Denonville's campaign against the Iroquois.

[2] Engagement of Tardiff to La Forêt" and Engagements to La Forêt," in Pease and Werner, *French Foundations*, 147-161.

theoretical more than actual. He did, however, establish the foundation of the Illinois trade by developing a working relationship with the tribes, convincing them to relocate in the Illinois Valley, and constructing the fort that became the distant Illinois Country French headquarters for trade and diplomacy. The structure was in place, but without the means to operate, La Salle could accomplish nothing.

Even though La Salle's fort had been abandoned, the legacy of the post was still alive decades later. In 1712, one group of Peoria Indians left Lake Peoria to establish new camps at Starved Rock, near and possibly within the decaying remains of old Fort St. Louis. Living among these Peoria were several French traders. It was at Starved Rock during this time that the Jesuit missionary Pierre-Gabriel Marest reestablished the Illinois mission in the Illinois Valley, that mission having been abandoned after the mortal wounding of Jesuit Jacques Gravier at the hands of a Peoria Indian at Lake Peoria, in 1705.

In 1722, pressure from Mesquakie war parties caused the Lake Peoria band to move alongside the Starved Rock Peoria. It was at this location that a French geological expedition led by François Philippe Renault, French superintendent of mines, found the two Peoria groups. Rumors of copper mines in the Illinois Valley brought the French group to Starved Rock. Although the precise origin of these rumors is uncertain, it is known that La Salle had written that copper had been found along the Illinois River. According to La Salle, "Mines [along the Illinois River] have not yet been seen although pieces of copper have been found in a number of places where the water is low."[3] It is also possible that La Salle's report of copper in the Illinois Valley induced another expedition, an English venture in 1773 under Patrick Kennedy, to again scour the valley for copper.[4]

In 1760, nearly seven decades after La Salle's fort had been abandoned by the French, Captain Sieur Passerat de la Chapelle led a contingent of 200 French-Canadian militia and Indians down the Illinois River. The group was bound for New Orleans after learning that Montreal had capitulated to the British several months earlier. After entering the Illinois Country, La Chapelle planned to establish winter quarters at La Salle's Fort St. Louis at Starved Rock, a site that he thought still existed. Climbing to the summit of the bluff, the French were disappointed to find that nothing remained of the fort. According to La Chapelle, it had been "burned a long time ago."[5] The French group then left the Rock and headed back upstream, about two miles, to today's Buffalo Rock where they began constructing a palisaded encampment called Fort Ottawa.

3 Ibid., 4.

4 Patrick Kennedy, "Mr. Patrick Kennedy's Journal up the Illinois River," *A Topographical Description of the Western Territory of North America,* ed. Gilbert Imlay (London: printed for J. Debrett, 1797), 510.

5 Passerat de La Chapelle, "La Chapelle's Remarkable Retreat Through the Mississippi Valley, 1760-1761," ed. Louise P. Kellogg, *Mississippi Valley Historical Review* (June 1935): 66.

Figure 24: Buffalo Rock as seen from the frozen Illinois River.
The Site of La Chapelle's Fort Ottawa, 1760-1761. Photo by the author.

While this fort was under construction, La Chapelle encountered a group of Peoria Indians who were wintering in the upper Illinois Valley (although the Illinois had not had summer villages in the Starved Rock area since at least 1741). As a gesture of friendship, La Chapelle gave the Peoria several gifts. The Peoria reciprocated by helping the French build the fort and by providing the French and their Native American allies with food. To improve relations between the French and the Peoria, La Chapelle set to work trying to learn the Illinois Indian language which, according to the French captain, "conciliated the good will" of one of their chiefs. The chief was so impressed that he presented La Chapelle with a "roll of skin" enclosed "in a sheath of wood." Unrolling the cylinder, La Chapelle saw words written in French, that read, "We Cavellier de la Salle, representing his Majesty, the king of France declare in his name a fair and perpetual alliance with the Nation of the Illinois. Cavellier de la Salle."[6] The document was authenticated, still bearing the badly worn imprint of La Salle's wax seal. Seizing the opportunity to impress the chief, La Chapelle told the Peoria leader that, like La Salle, he, too, represented the King of France and that he and his men "would always be faithful allies of his people." The chief, according to the officer, "declared that his ancestors had always respected this alliance and that his nation would continue it." La Chapelle then set his signature beneath that of La Salle. This incident clearly demonstrates La Salle's legacy, alliances the explorer had forged among the French and the Illinois back in 1680 were still very much intact in 1760.

---

[6] Ibid., 68.

Ironically, this event marks the end of both the French and the Illinois' occupation of the upper and central Illinois River Valley.

Filling the void left by the departing Peoria was a new Indian group, the Potawatomi, who by 1763 claimed the upper Illinois Valley as far as Starved Rock for their hunting grounds.[7] Living near the Potawatomi, at the Forks, were several French traders who, as late as 1790, were plying their trade in northeastern Illinois.[8] The French and Indian trade La Salle established in 1683 was still alive nearly a century after Fort St. Louis had been abandoned.

La Salle's legacy in the upper Illinois continues well into the nineteenth century. In 1867, the U.S. Army Corps of Engineers surveyed the Illinois River and drew what appears to be the first map of the stream to include latitude and longitude readings.

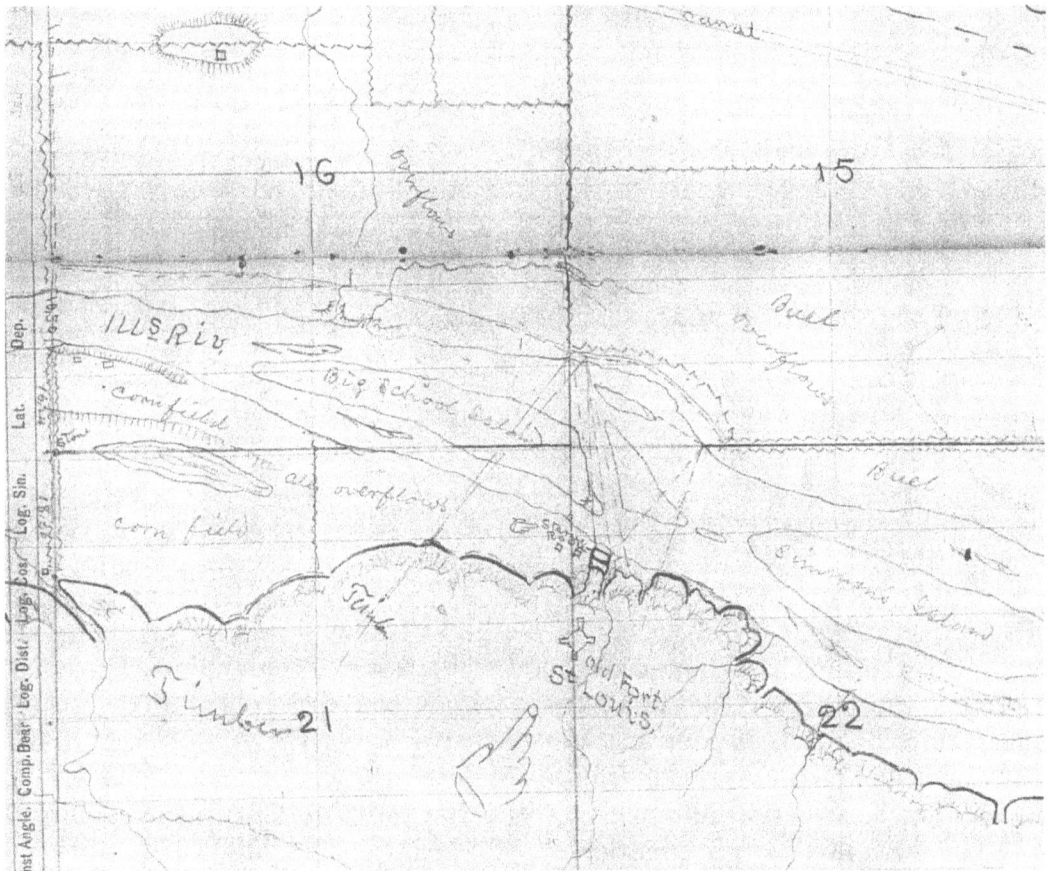

Figure 25: 1867 US Army Corps of Engineers map depicting Fort St. Louis at a site south of Starved Rock. Image courtesy of the US Army Corps of Engineers.

Negotiating the shallow Illinois River at today's Utica, Illinois, an anonymous engineer made note of the famous geological formation known today as "Starved Rock," La

---

[7] Anonymous, "Minutes of Mr. Hamburgh's Journal, 1763," *Travels in the American Colonies*, ed. Newton D. Mereness (New York: Macmillan Co., 1916), 359-364.

[8] Hugh Heward, *Hugh Heward's Journal from Detroit to the Illinois: 1790*, accessed February 23, 2013, http://archive.lib.msu.edu/MMM/JA/09/a/JA09a001p008.pdf.

Salle's Le Rocher. The corps map also includes a picture of a four-sided structure located a short distance behind Starved Rock, a site the cartographer called "Old Fort St. Louis."[9] While army engineers were mapping the river, Francis Parkman, the American historian, was nearby, researching his *La Salle and the Discovery of the Great West*. For more than a century, this book would be the definitive authority on La Salle and his enterprise in the Illinois Country.

La Salle's correspondences note that natural resources such as stone and coal were plentiful in the Illinois Country. In a letter to Canada Governor Frontenac, La Salle wrote: "There is excellent stone [?] and coal."[10] Another document reveals, "There are also a number of slate quarries and a quantity of coal." For more than a century, coal has been mined in Illinois. Today's villages of Standard, Cherry, Jonesville, Wenona, and a host of other towns located within 20 miles of Le Rocher were originally established as coal mining communities. Today, commercial limestone is extracted near Starved Rock at quarries owned by the Riverstone Group, Illinois Cement, Lafarge North America, and Buzzi Unicem USA. Silica sand is also quarried in pits near the Rock. In fact, one compelling reason for the state's purchase of Starved Rock as a public park was that the site itself, a sandstone bluff, could be destroyed and exploited. La Salle wrote in 1680 that these mineral resources were abundant in the Illinois Valley; today these places noted by La Salle provide employment for a multitude of people.

La Salle was, moreover, the first European to visualize and work toward a working line of communication between the Atlantic Ocean, Canada, the Great Lakes, and the Gulf of Mexico *via* the Illinois and Mississippi Rivers, and to make a substantial attempt at establishing these links. Although navigable from the Little Rock site (where d'Autray's land grant commenced) downstream, the Illinois River from present-day La Salle, Illinois to the Forks and beyond had historically been a navigational challenge fraught with impediments such as rapids and shallow water, especially during summer months. During the seventeenth-century, when the Illinois River was a much shallower stream, even simple shallow-draft watercraft such as the dugout canoe were unable to traverse this distance. For a century and a half after the time of La Salle, the Illinois River rapids and associated shallow waters were reported as being a navigational impediment for travelers, geological expeditions, and *voyageurs*. The reports, memoirs, and itineraries of Pierre Potier, Pierre-François Xavier de Charlevoix, Legardeur Delisle, Patrick Kennedy, Henry Schoolcraft, and others clear mention the rapids. Starved Rock was the effective head of navigation.

Eventually, a route to by-pass the Illinois rapids was constructed. Beginning at today's La Salle, Illinois and completed in 1848, the Illinois and Michigan Canal connected the Great Lakes *via* Chicago with markets and the resources of the Mississippi Valley. The canal had tremendous influence on the growth of Chicago and in the establishment and expansion of towns and cities that were built along it, notably

---

[9] "Old Fort St. Louis" appears to be an early reference to the "Newell Site," an archaeological anomaly that was destroyed by Jack and John Newell who dug for French and Indian artifacts at the location during the Great Depression.

[10] Pease and Werner, *French Foundations*, 4.

Joliet, Morris, and Ottawa. By the 1920s, construction had begun on a series of dams on the Illinois River where the rapids impeded river travel. Some of these projects included the Starved Rock Lock and Dam at Utica and the Marseilles Lock and Dam at Marseilles. In the early 1930s, other dams were built to facilitate commercial river traffic, including the Dresden Lock and Dam and the Peoria Lock and Dam. Another factor that greatly increased the viability of the Illinois River as a commercial trade and transport route was the reversal of the Chicago River, a project consisting of a series of canals that connected the Illinois River with Lake Michigan. The project routed water from the Chicago River that had once flowed into Lake Michigan instead into the canals and, ultimately, into the Illinois River. Consequently, the amount of water that flowed down the Illinois River vastly increased. Today's lock and dam system connecting Lake Michigan and the Illinois River—and, hence, the Mississippi Valley and the Gulf of Mexico—is but La Salle's vision of communication and trade between the Great Lakes and the Gulf realized.

Figure 26: The Illinois and Michigan Canal at La Salle, Illinois. Photo by the author.

In fact, the amount of material transported up and down the Illinois River today can be quantified to document that realization. Between 1683 and 1691, Fort St. Louis was headquarters for the Illinois fur trade. The islands in front of Starved Rock and 4.57 miles of the south shore of the river, as well as 20 square feet of the inside of the fort, belonged to d'Autray. Today, in front of La Salle's fort and attached to d'Autray's land is the Starved Rock Lock and Dam. According to figures provided by the United States Army Corps of Engineers, approximately 18,488,371 tons of cargo, primarily crude oil, petroleum products, chemicals, and agricultural commodities were transported through the locks in 2016. The cargo hauled by barges through the lock and dam system fuels the engine of progress which contributes to the quality of life that we enjoy today. La Salle's dreams of commerce, industry, and trade between the Great Lakes and the Gulf of Mexico were prescient indeed.

The names of Illinois towns such as La Salle, located in La Salle Township, which is located in La Salle County, Illinois, political subdivisions named for the explorer, testify to La Salle's endearing legacy as does the La Salle automobile, a vehicle called "the first of the smaller and more maneuverable luxury cars built to traditional standards," was manufactured by General Motors between 1927 and 1940.[11] The United State Navy commissioned two transport vessels USS La Salle, the first (AP-102) commissioned in 1943, and the second (LPD-3) commissioned in 1964, reclassified as Miscellaneous Command Ship (AGF-3) in 1972, and assigned as Commander, Sixth Fleet Flagship, in 1994. The latter USS La Salle, also known as the "Great White Ghost of the Arabian Coast," or the "Great White Target" because of its white exterior, was instrumental in the evacuation of 260 American and foreign national civilians at the beginning of the Iranian Hostage Crisis in 1979. On the ship's crest was the coat of arms of the La Salle family and an image of Fort Saint-Louis, La Salle's fort on top of today's Starved Rock.

Figure 27: Crest of the USS La Salle (AGF-3).
Notice the representation of La Salle's Fort St. Louis on the crest.
Photo courtesy of the US Navy.

Even though La Salle was unable to financially capitalize on the foundation of commerce that he laid, Chicago's La Salle Street, located in the heart of the city's financial district, speaks volumes about La Salle's vision of a commercial empire in the

---

[11] Motor Era, "1927-1940 La Salle," accessed August 8, 2016 at URL: http://www.motorera.com/lasalle/lasalle.htm.

West. La Salle's legacy is alive in today's Illinois as a working commercial hub, complete with viable transportation routes and places where trade, commerce, and industry, hallmarks of a modern world, have come to life. Although these accomplishments took centuries to develop, what La Salle envisioned is seen today from Canada to the Gulf of Mexico.

BIBLIOGRAPHY

Primary Sources

Baugy to La Durantaye, letter dated March 24, 1684, National Archives of Canada, Source RC 6515, call number MG1-Series C11A.

Blair, Emma Helen (ed.), *The Indian Tribes of the Upper Mississippi Valley and Region of the Great Lakes*, 2 vols. (Lincoln: University of Nebraska Press, 1996 version of copy originally published in 1911).

Cavelier de La Salle, from Portage de Chicagou, a' 30 Lieues des Fort St. Louis, 4 June 1683, Letter of, Houghton Library, Harvard College Library, call number MS Sparks 91.

Cavelier de La Salle to Jacques Bourdon d'Autray, deed in the French America Collection, Chicago History Museum Research Center.

Charlevoix, Pierre-Francis Xavier de, *Journal of a Voyage to North America*, 2 vols., ed. Louise Phelps Kellogg (Ann Arbor: University Microfilms, 1966).

Cox, Isaac Joslin (ed.), *The Journeys of Rene Robert Cavelier Sieur de La Salle*, 2 vols. (New York: Allerton Book Company, 1906).

Foster, William C. (ed.), *The La Salle Expedition to Texas: The Journal of Henri Joutel, 1684-1687* (Austin: Texas State Historical Association, 1998).

French, Benjamin Franklin (ed.), *Historical Collections of Louisiana*, part I (New York: Wiley and Putnam, 1846).

"Grant of La Salle to D'Autray, 1683," *Cavelier de La Salle to Jacques Bourdon d'Autray*, deed of in French America Collection, Chicago History Museum Research Center.

Hennepin, Louis, *A New Discovery of a Vast Country in America*, ed. Reuben Gold Thwaites, 2 vols. (Toronto: Coles Publishing, 1974).

Kellogg, Louise Phelps (ed.), *Early Narratives of the Northwest, 1634-1699* (New York: Scribner's Sons, 1917).

Margry, Pierre (ed.), Découvertes *et établissements des Français dans l'ouest et dans le sud de l'Amérique septentrionale, 1614-1754*, 6 vols. (Paris: Maisonneuve, 1876-1886).

O'Callaghan, Edmund Bailey (ed.), *Documents Relating to the Colonial History of New York*, ed. 15 volumes on CD (Saugerties, NY: Hope Farm Press, 2001 edition).

Pease, Theodore Calvin and Raymond C. Werner (eds.), *French Foundations*, Collections of the Illinois State Historical Library, vol. XXIII, French series Volume I (Springfield: Trustees of the Illinois State Historical Library, 1934).

Shea, John Dawson Gilmary (ed.), *Discovery and Exploration of the Mississippi Valley*, Elibron replica edition of 1852 work (Clinton Hall, New York: Redfield, 1852).

The French Regime in Wisconsin, I—1634-1727, Collections of the State Historical Society of Wisconsin, vol. XVI (Madison: State Historical Society of Wisconsin, 1902).

Thwaites, Reuben Gold (ed.), *Jesuit Relations and Allied Documents, 1610-1791* (Cleveland: Burrows, 1901).

Weddle, Robert S, Mary Morkovsky, and Patricia Galloway (eds.), *La Salle, the Mississippi, and the Gulf, Three Primary Documents* (College Station: Texas A&M University Press, 1987).

Secondary Sources

Alvord, Clarence Walworth, *The Illinois Country, 1673-1818* (Urbana and Chicago: University of Illinois Press, 1920).

Anderson, Melville B (trans), *Relations of the Discoveries and Voyages of Cavelier de La Salle from 1679 to 1681, The Official Narrative* (Chicago: Caxton Club, 1901).

------ *Relation of Henri de Tonty Concerning the Explorations of La Salle from 1678 to 1683* (Chicago: Caxton Club, 1898).

Balesi, Charles J., *The Time of the French in the Heart of North America, 1673-1818* (Chicago: Alliance Francaise, 1991).

Blasingham, Emily Jane, *The Illinois Indians, 1634-1800: A Study in Depopulation*, Ph.D. dissertation, 1956, Indiana University (University Microfilms, Ann Arbor, Michigan).

Bruseth, and James E. and Toni S. Turner, *From a Watery Grave, the Discovery and Excavation of La Salle's Shipwreck, La Belle* (College Station: Texas A&M University Press, 2005).

Campeau, "The Maps Relative to the Discovery of the Missisipi [sic] by Father Jacques Marquette and Louis Jolliet," in *Les Cahiers des Dix* (1992).

Delanglez, Jean, *Life and Voyages of Louis Jolliet (1645-1700)* (Chicago: Institute of Jesuit History, 1948).

Eccles, William J. *The Canadian Frontier 1534-1760* (Albuquerque: University of New Mexico Press, 1969).

Hamilton, Raphael N. S.J., *Marquette's Explorations: The Narratives Reexamined* (Madison: University of Wisconsin Press 1970).

Jablow, Joseph, *Indians of Illinois and Indiana* (New York: Garland Publishing, 1974).

Kinietz, Vernon W., *Indians of the Western Great Lakes 1615-1760* (Ann Arbor: University of Michigan Press, 1965).

Leavelle, Tracy Neal, *The Catholic Calumet* (Philadelphia: University of Pennsylvania Press, 2012).

McCafferty, Michael, *Native American Place Names in Indiana* (Urbana: University of Illinois Press, 2008).

Osler, E.B. *La Salle* (Don Mills, Ontario: Longman's Canada Limited, 1967).

Parkman, Francis, *La Salle and the Discovery of the Great West*, ed. Jon Krakauer (New York: Modern Library, 1999).

Temple, Wayne, *Indian Villages of the Illinois Country*. Illinois State Museum Scientific Papers, vol. II, part 2 (Springfield: Illinois State Museum, 1966).

Wedel, Mildred Mott, (ed.) *A Jean Delanglez Anthology* (New York: Garland Publishing 1985).

White, Sam, *A Cold Welcome: The Little Ice Age and Europe's Encounter with North America* (Cambridge: Harvard University Press, 2017).

Wiggers, Raymond, *Geology Underfoot in Illinois* (Missoula, MT: Mountain Press Company, 1997).

Zitomersky, Joseph, *French Americans: Native Americans in Eighteenth Century French Colonial Louisiana* (Lund, Sweden: Lund University Press, 1995).

Journal and Reference Articles

Burke-Gaffney, M. W., "Franquelin, Jean-Baptiste-Louis," *Dictionary of Canadian Biography*, vol. II (University of Toronto/Université Laval, 1969, revised 1982).

Delanglez, Jean, "The Voyages of Tonti in North America, 1678-1704," in *Mid–America, an Historical Review*, vol. 26, number 4 (October 1944).

Eccles, William J., "Brisay de Denonville, Jacques-René de, Marquis de Denonville," in *Dictionary of Canadian Biography*, vol. 2 (Toronto/Quebec: University of Toronto/Université Laval), 2003.

Garraghan, Gilbert J., SJ, "La Salle's Jesuit Days," Mid-America magazine XIX, 1937.

Grantham, Larry, "The Illini Village of the Marquette and Jolliet Voyage of 1673," in *The Missouri Archaeologist*, vol. 54, (1996).

Mazrim, Robert F. *Protohistory at the Grand village of the Kaskaskia, The Illinois Country on the Eve of Colony*, Studies in Archaeology no. 10 (Urbana: Illinois State Archaeological Survey, 2015.

Vachon, André, "Louis Jolliet," *Dictionary of Canadian Biography*, vol. I, 1000-1700 (Toronto: University of Toronto Press, 1979, revised 2017).

Wedel, Mildred Mott, "Peering at the Ioway Indians Through the Mist of Time; 1650 circa 1700," *The Journal of the Iowa Archaeological Society*, vol. 33 (1986).

Weilbrenner, Bernard, "Morel de La Durantaye, Oliver," in *Dictionary of Canadian Biography*, vol. II (Toronto: University of Toronto Press, 1969, rev. ed., 1982).

Web Sources

Campbell, Paul Brian, SJ "The Making of a Jesuit," in *People for Others*, November 13, 2008, accessed March 5, 2016 at URL: http://peopleforothers. loyolapress.com/ 2008/11/the-making-of-a-jesuit/.

Carlos, Ann and Frank Lewis, "Fur Trade (1670-1870)," *EH.Net Encyclopedia*, edited by Robert Whaples (March 16, 2008). URL http://eh.net/encyclopedia/the-economic-history-of-the-fur-trade-1670-to-1870/.

Catholic Encyclopedia, at URL: http://www.newadvent.org

Gingras, Frédéric, "Membré, Zenobé" in *Dictionary of Canadian Biography*, vol. 1, University of Toronto/Université Laval, 2003–, accessed November 6, 2018, http://www.biographi.ca/en/bio/membre_zenobe_1E.html

Goyau, Georges, "St. Louis IX," in *The Catholic Encyclopedia* (New York: Robert Appleton Company, 1910), accessed February 22, 2013, http://www.newadvent.org/cathen/09368a.htm.

Great Lakes Exploration accessed December 6, 2018, http://greatlakesexploration.org/expedition.htm.

Handbook of Texas Online, Robert S. Weddle, "Membré, Zenobé," 2010, accessed November 06, 2018, http://www.tshaonline.org/handbook/online/articles/fme70.

Historical Collections of Louisiana and Florida, Second Series (New York: Albert Mason, 1875), 4, accessed August 27, 2019, from https://archive.org/details/ historicalcolle06frengoog/page/n28.

Hodge, Frederick Webb (ed.), Handbook of American Indians North of Mexico, 2 parts (Washington: government printing office, 1907) II: 172, URL: https://archive.org/stream/handbookamindians01hodgrich#page/172/mode/2up.

Ignatian Spirituality, A Service of Loyola Press, accessed March 5, 2016 at URL: http://www.ignatianspirituality.com/ignatian-prayer/the-spiritual-exercises/what-are-the-spiritual-exercises.

Internet Archives: Digital Library of Free Books at URL: https://archive.org/index.php.

Library of Congress, 1675, 1684, and 1688 maps of Jean-Baptiste Franquelin accessed August 15, 2016 at URLs:
https://www.loc.gov/resource/g3300.ct000655/
https://www.loc.gov/resource/g3300.ct000656/
https://www.loc.gov/resource/g3300.ct000668/?r=0.314,0.335,0.166,0.065,0.

Lowery, Woodbury, *The Lowery Collection, A Descriptive List of Maps of the Spanish Possessions Within the Present Limits of the United States, 1502-1820* (Washington: Government Printing Office, 1912), 165, accessed August 30, 2016 at Internet Archives at URL: https://archive.org/details/lowery collection00lowerich/page .

Monet, J., Jacques Marquette, *Dictionary of Canadian Biography*, vol. 1, (University of Toronto/Université Laval, 1966 revised 1979) accessed November 4, 2018 at http://www.biographi.ca/en/bio/marquette_jacques_1E.html

Motor Era, accessed August 8, 2016, at URL: http://www.motorera.com/lasalle/lasalle.htm.

Wallace, W. Stewart, ed., The Encyclopedia of Canada, Vol. II, Toronto, University Associates of Canada, 1948, 411p., pp. 111-113. Accessed December 11, 2015 at URL: http://faculty.marianopolis.edu/c.belanger/quebechistory/encyclopedia/CompanyofNewFrance-QuebecHistory.htm.

Other Sources

Anonymous, U.S. Army Corps of Engineers map (1867).

Documents found in the *Miami Tribal History Document Series, Great Lakes - Ohio Valley Ethnohistory Collection, Erminie Wheeler-Voegelin Archives*, Indiana University, Bloomington.

Personal communications with Michael McCafferty, linguist at Indiana University, Bloomington.

Tucker, Sara Jones, *Indian Villages of the Illinois Country*, vol. II, scientific papers, Illinois State Museum, part I, Atlas (Springfield: 1942).

Woermann Maps, U.S. Army Corps of Engineers (1902-1904).

ABOUT THE AUTHOR

Mark Walczynski is Park Historian for the Starved Rock Educational and Historical Foundation located at Starved Rock State Park, Utica, Illinois. His work has been published in books and scholarly journals including the *Journal of the Illinois State Historical Society*; *Le Journal*, the journal of the Center for French Colonial Studies; *Michigan's Habitant Heritage*, the journal of the French-Canadian Heritage Society of Michigan; *American Indian Places: A Historical Guidebook* (Houghton Mifflin Co.); and other publications. He is also a contributor to the DVD *The Early History of the Illinois Indians*. *Inquietus, La Salle in the Illinois Country* is Mark's third book on Illinois history and second with the Center for French Colonial Studies. *Massacre 1769: The Search for the Origin of the Legend of Starved Rock* appeared in 2013. He is retired from the Illinois Department of Natural Resources and has taught college at Illinois Valley Community College in Oglesby, Illinois for nine years.

www.ingramcontent.com/pod-product-compliance
Lightning Source LLC
Chambersburg PA
CBHW081153090426

42736CB00017B/3298